Collins
My First
English-English-Bangla
Dictionary

ইংংলা

Exclusively Distributed in the Indian subcontinent by Ratna Sagar

HarperCollins Publishers
Westerhill Road
Bishopbriggs
Glasgow
G64 2QT

First edition 2011

Reprint 10 9 8 7 6 5 4 3 2 1 0

© HarperCollins Publishers 2011

ISBN 978-0-00-741563-2

Collins® is a registered trademark of HarperCollins Publishers Limited

www.collinslanguage.com

A catalogue record for this book is available from the British Library

Artwork and design by Q2A Media

Printed in India by Gopsons Papers Ltd

Images used under licence from Shutterstock.com

All rights reserved. No part of this book may be reproduced, stored in a retrieval system, or transmitted in any form or by any means, electronic, mechanical, photocopying, recording or otherwise, without the prior permission in writing of the Publisher. This book is sold subject to the conditions that it shall not, by way of trade or otherwise, be lent, re-sold, hired out or otherwise circulated without the publisher's prior consent in any form of binding or cover other than that in which it is published and without a similar condition including this condition being imposed on the subsequent purchaser.

Entered words that we have reason to believe constitute trademarks have been designated as such. However, neither the presence nor absence of such designation should be regarded as affecting the legal status of any trademark.

Editorial consultant
Suchita Singh
Formerly Co-ordinator, Lexical Build Project, Central Institute of Indian Languages

Translation co-ordination
Ajit Shirodkar

Translators
Prachi Banerjee
Gopal Chowdhury

Editors
Shalini Bansal
Suchitra Choudhury-Talukdar
Gerry Breslin
Lucy Cooper
Kerry Ferguson
Anne Robertson

Editor-in-chief
Dr Elaine Higgleton

এই অভিধানে কীভাবে শব্দ খুঁজতে হয়

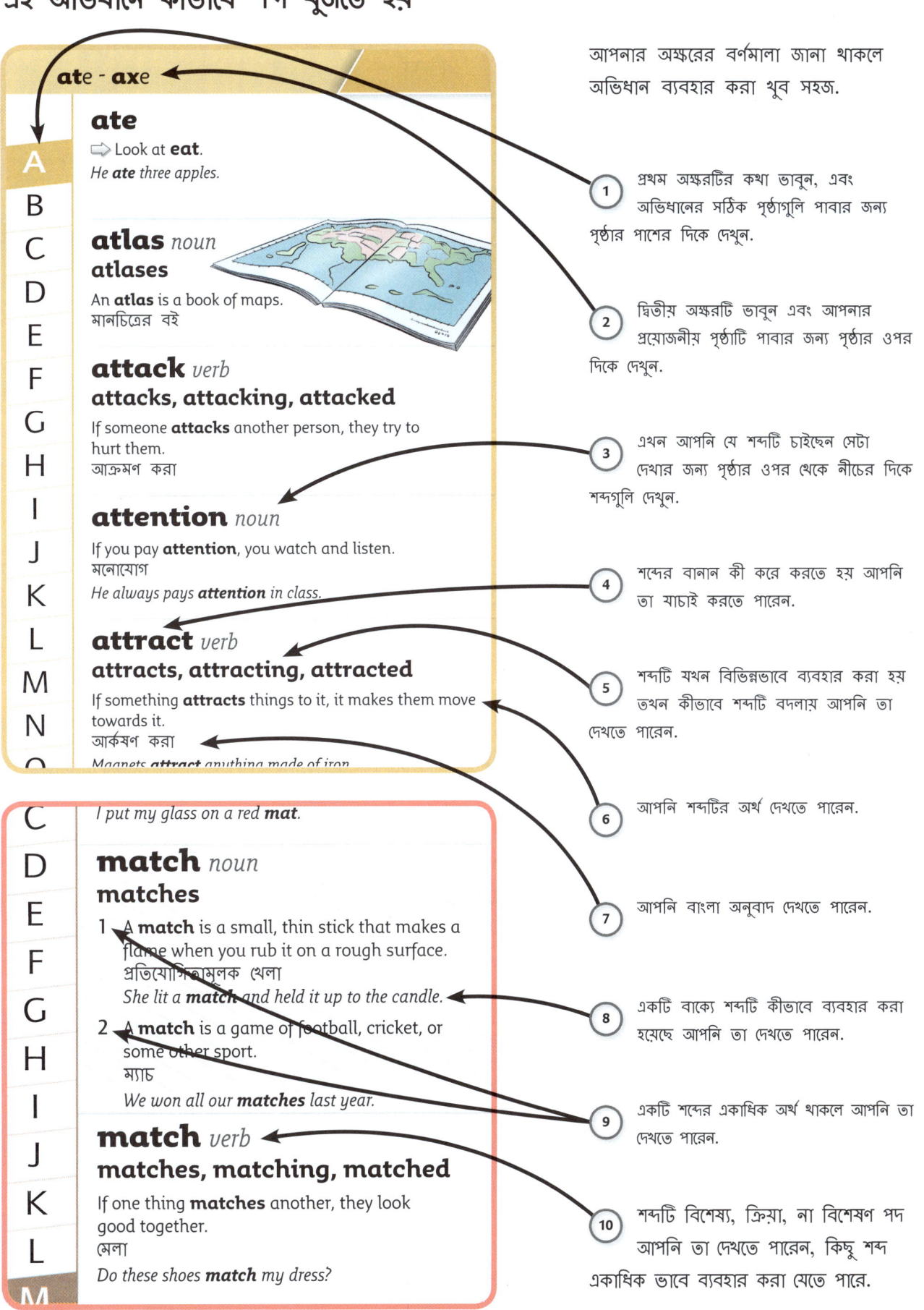

শব্দগুলি কীভাবে কাজ করে

বিশেষ্য

যে শব্দগুলি মানুষ, জায়গা বা জিনিসের বর্ণনা দেয় সেগুলি হল **বিশেষ্য**.

arm noun
bird noun
car noun

আপনার যদি একাধিক জিনিস থাকে, তাহলে আপনি যে শব্দ **-s** অক্ষর দিয়ে শেষ হয় সেটি ব্যবহার করেন.

arms
birds
cars

বিশেষণ

জিনিস, মানুষ বা জায়গা কী রকম **বিশেষণ** তার বর্ণনা দেয়.

happy adjective
wild adjective
wet adjective

বিশেষণ বিভিন্নভাবে ব্যবহার করা যেতে পারে.

happier, happiest
wilder, wildest
wetter, wettest

ক্রিয়া

ক্রিয়া হল সেই শব্দগুলি যেগুলি আপনি যা করেন তার বর্ণনা দেয়.

eat verb
cry verb
talk verb

ক্রিয়া বিভিন্নভাবে ব্যবহার করা যেতে পারে.

eats, eating, ate, eaten
cries, crying, cried
talks, talking, talked

আপনি এখন যা করছেন সেই বিষয়ে বলার জন্য **ক্রিয়া** ব্যবহার করা যেতে পারে.

*He **teaches** people how to play the piano.*
*He **is** in the school football team.*

আপনি অতীতে যে সব জিনিস করেছেন সেই বিষয়ে বলার জন্য ক্রিয়া ব্যবহার করা যেতে পারে.

*She **took** the plates into the kitchen.*
*She **talked** to him on the phone.*

আপনি ভবিষ্যতে কী করবেন সেই বিষয়েও ক্রিয়া ব্যবহার করা যেতে পারে.

*Mum **will** be angry.*
*Our teacher **will** give the prizes to the winners.*
***We'll** come along later.*

যে সুপরামর্শগুলি আপনাকে বানানে সাহায্য করবে!

অভিধানে আপনার আকাঙ্ক্ষিত শব্দটি পাবার পর, "Look, Say, Cover, Write, Check" কৌশল ব্যবহার করে কীভাবে বানান করতে হয় শেখার চেষ্টা করুন:

Look যত্নসহকারে শব্দটি দেখুন.
শব্দটির আকার ও দৈর্ঘ্য দেখুন.
শব্দটির অক্ষরগুলি দেখুন এবং অক্ষরগুলির কোন ধরণ আছে কী না দেখুন যা আপনাকে ভবিষ্যতে বানান করার জন্য মনে রাখতে সাহায্য করতে পারে, যেমন bright, light, tight.

Say শব্দটি জোরে বলুন.
শব্দটি উচ্চারণের কথা ভাবুন! আপনি কী এই রকম উচ্চারণের একটি শব্দের বানান করতে পারেন? আপনার শব্দটি কী এর উচ্চারণের মত? শব্দটি উচ্চারণ করুন এবং বানান করার চেষ্টা করুন.

Cover শব্দটি ঢাকুন যাতে আপনি দেখতে না পান.

Write অভিধানে শব্দটি না দেখে শব্দটি লিখুন. এটা করার সময় শব্দটি কী রকম দেখতে সেই বিষয়ে ভাবুন! এটা কী ঠিক দেখাচ্ছে? এর আকার কী সঠিক? এর দৈর্ঘ্য কী সঠিক মাপের?

Check আপনি যে সঠিকভাবে লিখেছেন তা যাচাই করুন.

Aa

abacus noun
abacuses
An **abacus** is a frame with beads that move along pieces of wire. It is used for counting.
অ্যাবাকাস

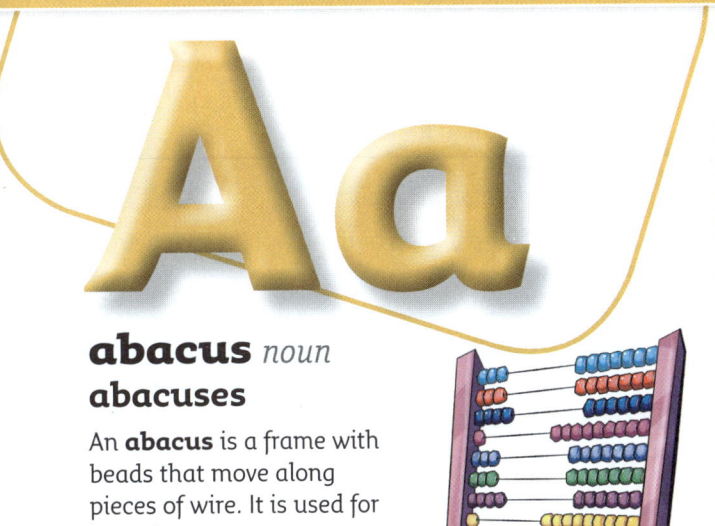

able
If you are **able** to do something, you know how to do it.
সক্ষম
*She is **able** to swim.*

about
1 **About** means to do with.
সম্বন্ধে
*This book is **about** history.*

2 **About** also means near to something.
প্রায়
*His grandfather is **about** 80 years old.*

above
If something is **above** another thing, it is over it or higher than it.
উপরে
*Lift the ball **above** your head.*

accident noun
accidents
1 An **accident** is something nasty that happens, and that hurts someone.
দুর্ঘটনা
*He broke his leg in a car **accident**.*

2 If something happens by **accident**, you do not expect it to happen.
দৈবক্রমে
*I dropped a cup by **accident**.*

ache verb
aches, aching, ached
If a part of your body **aches**, you feel a steady pain there.
যন্ত্রণা করা
*My leg **aches** a lot.*

acorn noun
acorns
An **acorn** is the seed of an oak tree.
ওকগাছের ফল

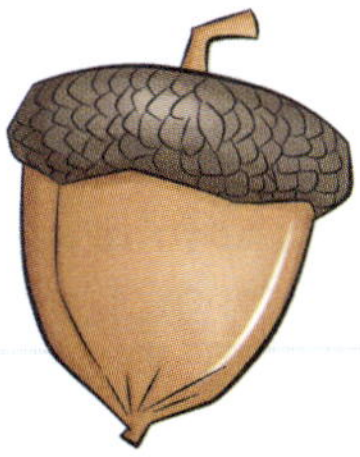

across
If someone goes **across** a place, they go from one side of it to the other.
আড়াআড়ি ভাবে
*She walked **across** the road.*

act verb
acts, acting, acted
1 When you **act**, you do something.
কাজ করা
*The police **acted** quickly to stop the fight.*

2 If you **act** in a play or film, you pretend to be one of the people in it.
অভিনয় করা

active adjective
Someone who is **active** moves around a lot.
সক্রিয়
*My grandmother is very **active** for her age.*

add verb
adds, adding, added
1 If you **add** one thing to another, you put it with the other thing.
মেশানো
Add the water to the flour.

2 If you **add** numbers together, you find out how many they make together.
যোগ করা
Add three and six.

address noun
addresses
Your **address** is the name of the place where you live.
ঠিকানা

adjective noun
adjectives
An **adjective** is a word like "big" or "beautiful", that tells you more about a person or thing.
বিশেষণ

1

admire verb
admires, admiring, admired

If you **admire** something, you like it and think that it is very nice or very good.
শ্রদ্ধা করা/প্রশংসা করা
I **admired** his painting.

adopt verb
adopts, adopting, adopted

If you **adopt** another person's child, you take them into your own family as your son or daughter.
দত্তক নেওয়া

adult noun
adults

An **adult** is a person who is not a child anymore.
প্রাপ্ত বয়স্ক

adventure noun
adventures

An **adventure** is something exciting which you do, or which happens to you.
রোমাঞ্চ
He wrote a book about his **adventures** in the jungle.

adverb noun
adverbs

An **adverb** is a word like "slowly", "now", or "very" that tells you about how something is done.
ক্রিয়ার বা বিশেষণের বিশেষণ

aeroplane noun
aeroplanes

An **aeroplane** is a large vehicle with wings and engines that flies through the air.
উড়োজাহাজ

afraid adjective

If you are **afraid**, you are frightened because you think that something bad will happen to you.
ভীত
I am not **afraid** of the dark.

after

1. If something happens **after** another thing, it happens later than it.
পরে
I watched television **after** dinner.

2. If you go **after** a person or thing, you follow them or chase them.
পিছনে
They ran **after** her.

afternoon noun
afternoons

The **afternoon** is the part of each day between twelve noon and about six o'clock.
অপরাহ্ন

again

If something happens **again**, it happens another time.
পুনরায়
We went to the park **again** yesterday.

against

1. If something is **against** another thing, it is touching it.
হেলান দেওয়া
He leaned **against** the wall.

2. If you play **against** someone in a game, you try to beat them.
বিপক্ষে
The two teams played **against** one another.

age noun
ages

Your **age** is the number of years that you have lived.
বয়স

ago

You use **ago** to talk about a time in the past.
আগে
She left two weeks **ago**.

agree - allow

agree verb
agrees, agreeing, agreed

If you **agree** with someone, you think the same as they do about something.
একমত হওয়া
I **agree** with you about him.

ahead
Someone who is **ahead** of another person is in front of them.
সামনে
My brother ran **ahead** of us.

air noun
Air is the mixture of gases all around us that we breathe.
বায়ু
I opened the window and let in some **air**.

aircraft noun
aircraft

An **aircraft** is any vehicle which can fly.
বিমান

airport noun
airports

An **airport** is a place where aeroplanes fly from and land.
বিমানবন্দর

alarm noun
alarms

An **alarm** is a piece of equipment that warns you of danger by making a noise.
সংকেতধ্বনি
The car **alarm** woke us up.

alien noun
aliens

In stories and films, an **alien** is a creature from another planet.
অন্য গ্রহের প্রাণী

alike adjective
If people or things are **alike**, they are the same in some way.
এক সমান
The two cats looked **alike**.

alive adjective
If a person, an animal or a plant is **alive**, they are living and not dead.
জীবিত

all
You use **all** to talk about everything, everyone, or the whole of something.
সমস্ত
Did you eat **all** of it?

alligator noun
alligators

An **alligator** is a large reptile with a long body, a long mouth and sharp teeth. **Alligators'** mouths are in the shape of a letter U.
কুমির প্রজাতির

allow verb
allows, allowing, allowed

If you **allow** someone to do something, you let them do it.
অনুমতি দেওয়া
Mum **allowed** us to go out and play.

3

all right - amphibian

all right or alright adjective
If you say that something is **all right**, you mean that it is good enough.
ঠিক আছে
I thought the film was **all right**.

almost
Almost means very nearly.
প্রায়
I **almost** missed the bus.

alone adjective
When you are **alone**, you are not with any other people.
একা
She was **alone** in the room.

along
1 If you walk **along** a road or other place, you move towards one end of it.
বরাবর
We walked **along** the street.

2 If you bring something **along** when you go somewhere, you bring it with you.
সঙ্গে
She brought a present **along** to the party.

aloud
When you read or talk **aloud**, you read or talk so that other people can hear you.
উচ্চস্বরে
She read the story **aloud** to us.

alphabet noun
alphabets
An **alphabet** is a set of letters that is used for writing words. The letters are arranged in a special order.
বর্ণমালা
A is the first letter of the **alphabet**.

already
You use **already** to show that something has happened before the present time.
ইতিমধ্যে
She is **already** here.

also
You use **also** to give more information about something.
এছাড়াও
I'm cold, and I'm **also** hungry.

always
If you **always** do something, you do it every time or all the time.
সর্বদা
She's **always** late for school.

am
⇨ Look at **be**.
I **am** six years old.

amazing adjective
You say that something is **amazing** when it is a surprise and you like it.
বিস্ময়কর
We had an **amazing** holiday.

ambulance noun
ambulances
An **ambulance** is a vehicle for taking people to hospital.
অ্যামবুলেন্স

amount noun
amounts
An **amount** of something is how much there is of it.
পরিমাণ/ টাকার অঙ্কের পরিমাণ
We only have a small **amount** of food.

amphibian noun
amphibians
An **amphibian** is an animal that lives both on land and in water, for example a frog or a toad.
উভয়চর প্রাণী

frog

4

ancient - **an**ything

ancient *adjective*

Ancient means very old, or from a long time ago.
প্রাচীনকালের,
They lived in an **ancient** castle.

angry *adjective*
angrier, angriest

When you are **angry**, you feel very upset about something.
ক্রুদ্ধ
She was **angry** at her brother for breaking the window.

animal *noun*
animals

An **animal** is any creature that is alive, but not a plant or a person.
জন্তু

ankle *noun*
ankles

Your **ankle** is the part of your body where your foot joins your leg.
গোড়ালি
I fell and twisted my **ankle**.

annoy *verb*
annoys, annoying, annoyed

If something **annoys** you, it makes you angry and upset.
বিরক্ত
It **annoys** me when people are rude.

another

You use **another** to mean one more.
অন্য একটি
She ate **another** cake.

answer *verb*
answers, answering, answered

If you **answer** someone, you say something back to them.
উত্তর দেওয়া
She said hello, but he didn't **answer**.

ant *noun*
ants

Ants are small insects that live in large groups.
পিঁপড়ে

antelope *noun*
antelopes

An **antelope** is an animal that looks like a deer.
কৃষ্ণসার হরিন

any

1 You use **any** to mean some of a thing.
কোন
Is there **any** juice left?

2 You also use **any** to show that it does not matter which one.
যে কোন
Take **any** book you want.

anybody

You use **anybody** to talk about a person, when it does not matter which one.
যে কেউ
Is there **anybody** there?

anyone

You use **anyone** to talk about a person, when it does not matter who.
কাউকে
Don't tell **anyone**.

anything

You use **anything** to talk about a thing, when it does not matter which one.
যে কোন জিনিস
I can't see **anything**.

anywhere

You use **anywhere** to talk about a place, when it does not matter which one.
যে কোন জায়গায়
You can go **anywhere** you like.

apart

1 When things are **apart**, there is a space or a distance between them.
ব্যবধানে
The desks are too far **apart**.

2 If you take something **apart**, you take it to pieces.
খুলে ফেলা
He took his bike **apart**.

ape noun
apes

An **ape** is an animal like a large monkey with long, strong arms and no tail.
বনমানুষ

apologize
or **apologise** verb
apologizes, apologizing, apologized

When you **apologize**, you say that you are sorry for something you have said or done.
ক্ষমা চাওয়া
He **apologized** for breaking the window.

appear verb
appears, appearing, appeared

When something **appears**, it becomes possible to see it.
দৃশ্যমান হওয়া
The sun **appeared** from behind the clouds.

apple noun
apples

An **apple** is a firm, round fruit with green, red, or yellow skin.
আপেল

April noun

April is the month after March and before May. It has 30 days.
এপ্রিল
His birthday is in **April**.

apron noun
aprons

An **apron** is a large piece of cloth that you wear over your other clothes to keep them clean when you are cooking or painting.
বস্ত্র-রক্ষিণী

are

➪ Look at **be**.
They **are** both in my class.

area noun
areas

An **area** is a part of a place.
অঞ্চল
We live in an **area** near the park.

aren't

Aren't is short for **are not**.
My friends **aren't** here today.

argue verb
argues, arguing, argued

If you **argue** with someone, you talk about something that you do not agree about.
বাদানুবাদ করা
We **argued** about where to go.

argument noun
arguments

If you have an **argument** with someone, you talk about something that you do not agree about.
তর্কবিতর্ক
She had an **argument** with another girl.

arm - **as**tronaut

arm noun
arms

Your **arms** are the two parts of your body between your shoulders and your hands.
বাহু
She stretched her **arms** out.

arm

armchair noun
armchairs

An **armchair** is a big comfortable chair with parts on the sides for you to put your arms on.
হাতলযুক্ত কেদারা

army noun
armies

An **army** is a large group of soldiers who fight in a war.
সেনাবাহিনী

around

1 **Around** means in a circle.
চারপাশে
There were lots of people **around** her.

2 You also use **around** to say that something is in every part of a place.
চারিধারে
His toys lay **around** the room.

3 **Around** also means near to something.
প্রায়
We left **around** noon.

arrange verb
arranges, arranging, arranged

1 If you **arrange** something, you make plans for it to happen.
আয়োজন করা
We **arranged** a party for her birthday.

2 If you **arrange** things somewhere, you put them in a way that looks tidy or pretty.
সাজিয়ে রাখা
He **arranged** the books in piles.

arrive verb
arrives, arriving, arrived

When you **arrive** at a place, you get there.
পৌঁছে যাওয়া
We **arrived** ten minutes late.

arrow noun
arrows

1 An **arrow** is a long, thin stick with a sharp point at one end.
তীর
The soldiers used bows and **arrows**.

2 An **arrow** is also a sign that shows you which way to go.
তীরচিহ্ন
Follow the **arrows** along the path.

art noun

Art is something that someone has made for people to look at, for example a painting or drawing.
চারুকলা

ask verb
asks, asking, asked

1 If you **ask** someone a question, you say that you want to know something.
জিজ্ঞাসা করা
I **asked** him what his name was.

2 If you **ask** for something, you say that you want it.
চাওয়া
She **asked** for some sweets.

asleep adjective

If you are **asleep**, you are sleeping.
ঘুমন্ত
The cat was **asleep** under the tree.

assembly noun
assemblies

An **assembly** is a group of people who meet together.
সভা
We were late for school **assembly**.

assistant noun
assistants

An **assistant** is someone who helps another person in their work.
সহায়ক

astronaut noun
astronauts

An **astronaut** is a person who travels in space.
মহাকাশচারী

a
b
c
d
e
f
g
h
i
j
k
l
m
n
o
p
q
r
s
t
u
v
w
x
y
z

7

ate - axe

ate
➩ Look at **eat**.
He **ate** three apples.

atlas noun
atlases

An **atlas** is a book of maps.
মানচিত্রের বই

attack verb
attacks, attacking, attacked

If someone **attacks** another person, they try to hurt them.
আক্রমণ করা

attention noun

If you pay **attention**, you watch and listen.
মনোযোগ
He always pays **attention** in class.

attract verb
attracts, attracting, attracted

If something **attracts** things to it, it makes them move towards it.
আকর্ষণ করা
Magnets **attract** anything made of iron.

audience noun
audiences

An **audience** is all of the people who watch or listen to something, for example a film or a play.
দর্শকবৃন্দ

August noun

August is the month after July and before September. It has 31 days.
আগস্ট মাস
We went on holiday in **August**.

aunt noun
aunts

Your **aunt** is the sister of your mother or father, or the wife of your uncle.
মাসি/পিসি/কাকিমা/জেঠিমা

author noun
authors

An **author** is a person who writes books.
লেখক

autumn noun
autumns

Autumn is the season after summer and before winter. In the **autumn** the weather usually becomes cooler and the leaves fall off the trees.
শরৎকাল

awake adjective

Someone who is **awake** is not sleeping.
জাগ্রত
I stayed **awake** until midnight.

away

1 If someone moves **away** from a place, they move so that they are not there any more.
চলে যাওয়া
He walked **away** from the house.

2 If you put something **away**, you put it where it should be.
সরিয়ে রাখা
Put your books **away** before you go.

awful adjective

If something is **awful**, it is very bad.
প্রচন্ড
There was an **awful** smell.

axe noun
axes

An **axe** is a tool with a handle and a big, sharp blade. It is used to chop wood.
কুঠার

8

Bb

baby *noun*
babies

A **baby** is a very young child.
শিশু

back *noun*
backs

1 Your **back** is the part of your body from your neck to your bottom.
পিঠ
*He was lying on his **back** in the grass.*

2 The **back** of something is the side or part of it that is farthest from the front.
পিছনে
*She was in a room at the **back** of the shop.*

backwards

1 If you move **backwards**, you move in the direction behind you.
পিছনের দিকে
*She walked **backwards**.*

2 If you do something **backwards**, you do it the opposite of the usual way.
উল্টোদিকে
*He had his jumper on **backwards**.*

bad *adjective*
worse, worst

1 Something that is **bad** is not nice or good.
খারাপ
*The weather is **bad** today.*

2 Someone who is **bad** does things they should not do.
মন্দ
*Some **bad** boys stole the money.*

badge *noun*
badges

A **badge** is a small piece of metal or plastic with words or a picture on it that you wear on your clothes.
ব্যাজ/চিহ্ন

badger *noun*
badgers

A **badger** is an animal that has a white head with two black stripes on it. **Badgers** live beneath the ground and come out at night.
একজাতীয় ক্ষুদ্র নিশাচর প্রাণী

bag *noun*
bags

A **bag** is a container that you use to hold or carry things.
ব্যাগ/থলে
*He put his shoes in his **bag**.*

bake *verb*
bakes, baking, baked

When you **bake** food, you cook it in an oven.
সেঁকা

baker *noun*
bakers

A **baker** is a person who makes and sells bread and cakes.
রুটিওয়ালা

balance *verb*
balances, balancing, balanced

When you **balance** something, you keep it steady and do not let it fall.
ভারসাম্য
*She **balanced** a book on her head.*

ball *noun*
balls

A **ball** is a round thing that you kick, throw or catch in games.
বল

ballet *noun*

Ballet is a kind of dance with special steps that often tells a story.
ব্যালে নৃত্য

balloon - bat

A B C D E F G H I J K L M N O P Q R S T U V W X Y Z

balloon noun
balloons

A **balloon** is a small bag made of thin rubber that you blow into to make it bigger.
বেলুন

banana noun
bananas

A **banana** is a long curved fruit with a thick yellow skin.
কলা

band noun
bands

1 A **band** is a group of people who play music together.
ব্যান্ড
He plays the guitar in a **band**.

2 A **band** is also a narrow strip of material that you put around something.
ফেট্টি
She wore a **band** round her hair.

bandage noun
bandages

A **bandage** is a long strip of cloth that you wrap around a part of your body when you have hurt it.
পট্টি

bang noun
bangs

A **bang** is a sudden, loud noise.
আচমকা জোরালো আওয়াজ
The balloon burst with a **bang**.

bank noun
banks

1 A **bank** is a place where people can keep their money.
ব্যাঙ্ক
He got some money from the **bank**.

2 A **bank** is also the ground beside a river.
নদীর পাড়
We walked along the **bank**.

bar noun
bars

A **bar** is a long, thin piece of wood or metal.
গরাদ
There were **bars** on the windows.

bare adjective
barer, barest

1 If a part of your body is **bare**, it is not covered by any clothes.
খালি
Her feet were **bare**.

2 If something is **bare**, it has nothing on top of it or inside it.
ফাঁকা
The cupboard was **bare**.

bark verb
barks, barking, barked

When a dog **barks**, it makes a short, loud noise.
কুকুরের ঘেউ ঘেউ করা

barn noun
barns

A **barn** is a big building on a farm where animals and crops are kept.
গোলাবাড়ি

base noun
bases

The **base** of something is the lowest part of it, or the part that it stands on.
ভিত
She stood at the **base** of the stairs.

basket noun
baskets

A **basket** is a container that you use to hold or carry things. It is made from thin strips of material.
ঝুড়ি

bat noun
bats

1 A **bat** is a special stick that you use to hit a ball in some games.
ব্যাট

2 A **bat** is also a small animal that looks like a mouse with wings. **Bats** come out to fly at night.
বাদুড়

bath noun
baths
A **bath** is a long container that you fill with water and sit in to wash yourself.
স্নানের পাত্র

bathroom noun
bathrooms
A **bathroom** is a room with a bath or shower in it.
স্নানঘর

battery noun
batteries
A **battery** is a small tube or box for storing electricity. You put **batteries** in things like toys and radios to make them work.
ব্যাটারী
*The clock needs a new **battery**.*

be verb
am, is, are, being, was, were, been
1. You use **be** to say what a person or thing is like.
   হওয়া
   *She **is** very young.*
2. You also use **be** to say that something is there.
   থাকা
   *There **is** a tree in the garden.*

beach noun
beaches
A **beach** is the land by the edge of the sea. It is covered with sand or stones.
সমুদ্রতট

bead noun
beads
A **bead** is a small piece of glass, wood or plastic with a hole through the middle. You put **beads** on a string to make necklaces or bracelets.
জপমালা

beak noun
beaks
A bird's **beak** is the hard part of its mouth.
পাখির ঠোঁট

bean noun
beans
A **bean** is the small seed of some plants that you can eat as a vegetable.
বীন/শুঁটিযুক্ত ফলধারী লতা

bear noun
bears
A **bear** is a big, strong animal with thick fur and sharp claws.
ভাল্লুক

beard noun
beards
A **beard** is the hair that grows on a man's chin and cheeks.
দাড়ি

beat verb
beats, beating, beat, beaten
1. If you **beat** something, you keep hitting it.
   মারা
   *He **beat** the drum with a stick.*
2. If you **beat** someone in a game or a competition, you do better than they do.
   হারিয়ে দেওয়া
   *He **beat** me in the race.*

beautiful adjective
If something is **beautiful**, it is very nice to look at or to listen to.
সুন্দর
*He painted a **beautiful** picture.*

became
➡ Look at **become**.
*She **became** very angry.*

because - behind

because
You use **because** to say why something happens.
কারণ
I went to bed **because** I was tired.

become verb
becomes, becoming, became, become
If one thing **becomes** another thing, it starts to be that thing.
পরিণত
The weather **became** cold.

bed noun
beds
A **bed** is a piece of furniture that you lie on when you sleep.
বিছানা

bedroom noun
bedrooms
A **bedroom** is a room with a bed in it where you sleep.
শোয়ার ঘর

bedtime noun
bedtimes
Your **bedtime** is the time when you usually go to bed.
শোওয়ার সময়
My **bedtime** is at eight o'clock.

bee noun
bees
A **bee** is an insect with wings and black and yellow stripes on its body. **Bees** live in large groups and make honey.
মৌমাছি

been
⇨ Look at **be**.
We have always **been** good friends.

beetle noun
beetles
A **beetle** is an insect with hard wings that cover its body when it is not flying.
গোবরে-পোকা

before
If one thing happens **before** another thing, it happens earlier than it.
আগে
My birthday is just **before** his.

began
⇨ Look at **begin**.
She **began** to laugh.

begin verb
begins, beginning, began, begun
If you **begin** to do something, you start to do it.
আরম্ভ করা
You can **begin** to write now.

begun
⇨ Look at **begin**.
He has **begun** to play the piano.

behave verb
behaves, behaving, behaved
1 The way you **behave** is the way that you do and say things.
আচরণ করা
She **behaves** like a baby.

2 If you **behave** yourself, you are good.
ভালো আচরণ করা
You can come if you **behave** yourself.

behind
If something is **behind** another thing, it is at the back of it.
পিছনে
He stood **behind** his desk.

12

believe verb
believes, believing, believed

If you **believe** something, you think that it is true.
বিশ্বাস করা
*I don't **believe** that story.*

bell noun
bells

A **bell** is a piece of metal in the shape of a cup that rings when you shake it or hit it.
ঘন্টা

belong verb
belongs, belonging, belonged

1. If something **belongs** to you, it is yours.
কারোর নিজের হওয়া
*The book **belongs** to her.*

2. If you **belong** to a group of people, you are one of them.
কোন কিছুর অন্তর্ভুক্ত
*He **belongs** to our team.*

3. If something **belongs** somewhere, that is where it should be.
যথাস্থানে থাকা
*Your toys **belong** in your room.*

below

If something is **below** another thing, it is lower down than it.
নমিন/নীচে/তলায়
*His shoes were **below** his bed.*

belt noun
belts

A **belt** is a band of leather or cloth that you wear around your waist.
বেল্ট

bench noun
benches

A **bench** is a long seat that two or more people can sit on.
বেঞ্চ

bend verb
bends, bending, bent

When you **bend** something, you change its shape so that it is not straight any more.
বেঁকানো
***Bend** your legs when you do this exercise.*

beneath

If something is **beneath** another thing, it is below it.
তলায়
*The dog was **beneath** the table.*

bent

⇨ Look at **bend**.
*He **bent** to pick up the bags.*

berry noun
berries

A **berry** is a small, soft fruit that grows on a bush or a tree.
কালোজাম

beside

If something is **beside** another thing, it is next to it.
পাশে
*He sat down **beside** me.*

best

If you say that something is **best**, you mean that it is better than all the others.
সর্বশ্রেষ্ঠ
*You are my **best** friend.*

better - **bl**ade

better

1 You use **better** to mean that a thing is very good compared to another thing.
উৎকৃষ্টতর
*His painting is **better** than mine.*

2 If you feel **better**, you do not feel ill any more.
সুস্থ বোধ করা
*I feel much **better** today.*

between

If you are **between** two things, one of them is on one side of you and the other is on the other side.
মধ্যে
*She stood **between** her two brothers.*

bicycle noun
bicycles

A **bicycle** is a vehicle with two wheels. You push the pedals with your feet to make the wheels turn.
বাইসাইকেল

big adjective
bigger, biggest

A person or thing that is **big** is large in size.
বিরাট
*She lives in a **big** house.*

bike noun
bikes

A **bike** is a bicycle or motorbike.
বাইক

bin noun
bins

A **bin** is a container that you put rubbish in.
আবর্জনা ফেলার পাত্র

bird noun
birds

A **bird** is an animal with feathers, wings, and a beak. Most **birds** can fly.
পাখি

birthday noun
birthdays

Your **birthday** is the date that you were born.
জন্মদিন
*She gave me a present on my **birthday**.*

biscuit noun
biscuits

A **biscuit** is a kind of small, hard, dry cake.
বিস্কুট

bit noun
bits

A **bit** of something is a small amount of it, or a small part of it.
অল্প
*I ate a **bit** of bread.*

bite verb
bites, biting, bit, bitten

If you **bite** something, you use your teeth to cut into it.
কামড়ানো
*The dog tried to **bite** him.*

black noun

Black is the colour of the sky at night.
কালো
*The car is **black**.*

blackboard noun
blackboards

A **blackboard** is a flat, black surface that you write on with chalk in a classroom.
ব্ল্যাকবোর্ড

blade noun
blades

A **blade** is the flat, sharp part of a knife that you use to cut things.
ব্লেড

blame verb
blames, blaming, blamed

If you **blame** someone for something bad, you think that they made it happen.
দোষারোপ করা
Mum **blamed** me for making the mess.

blanket noun
blankets

A **blanket** is a large, thick piece of cloth that you put on a bed to keep you warm.
কম্বল

blew
⇨ Look at **blow**.
The wind **blew** outside.

blind adjective
Someone who is **blind** cannot see.
অন্ধ

block noun
blocks

A **block** of something is a large piece of it with straight sides.
থণ্ড
We made a house with **blocks** of wood.

blood noun
Blood is the red liquid that moves around inside your body.
রক্ত

blouse noun
blouses

A **blouse** is something a girl or woman can wear. It covers the top part of the body and has buttons down the front.
ব্লাউজ

blow verb
blows, blowing, blew, blown

1. When the wind **blows**, it moves the air.
প্রবাহিত হওয়া

2. When you **blow**, you push air out of your mouth.
ফুঁ দেওয়া
He **blew** on his hands to keep them warm.

blue noun
Blue is the colour of the sky on a sunny day.
নীল
Her dress is **blue**.

blunt adjective
blunter, bluntest

Something that is **blunt** does not have a sharp point or edge.
ভোঁতা
My pencil is **blunt**.

boat noun
boats

A **boat** is a small vehicle that carries people on water.
নৌকা

body noun
bodies

A person's or animal's **body** is all their parts.
দেহ
It's fun to stretch and twist your **body**.

boil verb
boils, boiling, boiled

1. When water **boils**, it becomes very hot, and you can see bubbles in it and steam coming from it.
ফোটা

2. When you **boil** food, you cook it in water that is boiling.
ফোটানো

bone noun
bones

Your **bones** are the hard parts inside your body.
হাড়
I broke a **bone** in my leg.

blame - bone

a
b
c
d
e
f
g
h
i
j
k
l
m
n
o
p
q
r
s
t
u
v
w
x
y
z

15

bonfire - bow

A
B
C
D
E
F
G
H
I
J
K
L
M
N
O
P
Q
R
S
T
U
V
W
X
Y
Z

bonfire noun
bonfires

A **bonfire** is a big fire that is made outside.
কুটোর আগুন

book noun
books

A **book** is a set of pages with words or pictures on them, that are held together inside a cover.
বই

boot noun
boots

A **boot** is a kind of shoe that covers your foot and the lower part of your leg.
জুতো

bored adjective

If you are **bored**, you feel annoyed because you have nothing to do.
একঘেঁয়েমি

boring adjective

If something is **boring**, it is not interesting.
বিরক্তিকর

born verb

When a baby is **born**, it comes out of its mother's body.
জন্মগ্রহণ করা
My sister was **born** three years ago.

borrow verb
borrows, borrowing, borrowed

If you **borrow** something from someone, they let you have it for a short time and then you give it back.
ধার করা
Can I **borrow** your pen, please?

both

You use **both** to mean two people or two things together.
উভয়
He put **both** books into the drawer.

bottle noun
bottles

A **bottle** is a container made of glass or plastic that holds liquid.
বোতল

bottom noun
bottoms

1 The **bottom** of something is its lowest part.
তলদেশ

2 Your **bottom** is the part of your body that you sit on.
নিতম্ব

bought
⇨ Look at **buy**.
We **bought** bread and milk.

bounce verb
bounces, bouncing, bounced

When something **bounces**, it hits another thing and then moves away from it again.
লাফানো
The ball **bounced** across the floor.

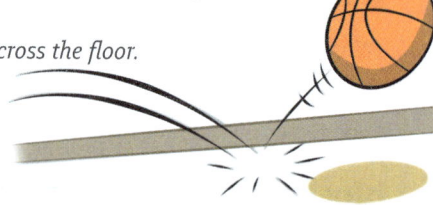

bow verb
bows, bowing, bowed

When you **bow**, you bend your body towards someone as a polite way of saying hello or thanking them.
মাথা ঝোঁকানো
They all **bowed** to the king.

bow noun
bows

1 A **bow** is a knot with two loose ends that you use to tie laces and ribbons.
টাই অথবা রীবনের গিঁট

2 A **bow** is also a long, curved piece of wood with a string stretched between the two ends, that is used to send arrows through the air.
ধনুক

16

bowl - bride

bowl noun
bowls

A **bowl** is a round container that you use to hold food or drink.
পাত্র

box noun
boxes

A **box** is a container with a hard, straight bottom and sides, and usually a lid.
বাক্স

boy noun
boys

A **boy** is a male child.
বালক

bracelet noun
bracelets

A **bracelet** is a chain or a band that you wear around your wrist.
কবজি-বন্ধনী

brain noun
brains

Your **brain** is inside your head. It controls your body and lets you think and feel things.
মস্তিষ্ক

branch noun
branches

The **branches** of a tree are the parts that grow out from its trunk and have leaves on them.
শাখা

brave adjective
braver, bravest

If you are **brave**, you are not afraid of something dangerous.
সাহসী

bread noun

Bread is a food that is made from flour and water and baked in an oven.
পাউরুটি

break verb
breaks, breaking, broke, broken

1 When something **breaks**, it goes into pieces.
ভেঙে যাওয়া
I dropped a plate and it **broke**.

2 When a machine **breaks**, it stops working.
অকেজো হয়ে যাওয়া
My brother **broke** the television.

breakfast noun
breakfasts

Breakfast is the first meal of the day.
প্রাতঃরাশ

breathe verb
breathes, breathing, breathed

When you **breathe**, air goes in and out of your body through your nose or your mouth.
নিঃশ্বাস নেওয়া

brick noun
bricks

Bricks are small blocks of baked earth used for building.
ইট

bride noun
brides

A **bride** is a woman who is getting married.
বিয়ের কনে

17

bridegroom - brush

bridegroom noun
bridegrooms

A **bridegroom** is a man who is getting married.
বর

bridge noun
bridges

A **bridge** is something that is built over a river, a road, or a railway so that people can get across it.
সেতু

bright adjective
brighter, brightest

1 A **bright** colour is very easy to see.
উজ্জ্বল
*She wore a **bright** red dress.*

2 Something that is **bright** shines with a lot of light.
ঝলমলে
*The sun is very **bright** today.*

brilliant adjective

Something that is **brilliant** is very good.
চমৎকার
*I thought the film was **brilliant**.*

bring verb
brings, bringing, brought

If you **bring** something, you take it with you when you go somewhere.
বহন করা
*You can **bring** a friend to the party.*

broke
⇨ Look at **break**.
*I'm sorry I **broke** the radio.*

broken adjective

If something is **broken**, it is in pieces.
ভাঙা
*All of his toys are **broken**.*

broom noun
brooms

A **broom** is a brush with a long handle that you use to sweep the floor.
ঝাড়ু

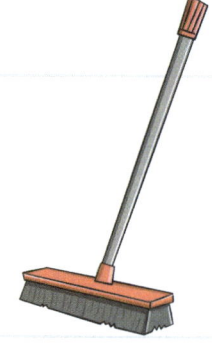

brother noun
brothers

Your **brother** is a boy or a man who has the same mother and father as you do.
ভাই

brought
⇨ Look at **bring**.
*We **brought** some food for the picnic.*

brown noun

Brown is the colour of earth or wood.
বাদামী
*Her eyes are dark **brown**.*

bruise noun
bruises

A **bruise** is a purple mark on your skin that appears if something hits a part of your body.
কালসিটে
*She has a big **bruise** on her leg.*

brush noun
brushes

A **brush** has lots of short hairs fixed to a handle. You use a **brush** to make your hair tidy, to clean things, or to paint.
ব্রাশ

bubble noun
bubbles
A **bubble** is a small ball of liquid with air inside it.
বুদ্বুদ্

bucket noun
buckets
A **bucket** is a deep, round container with a handle that you use to hold or carry liquids.
বালতি

buckle noun
buckles
A **buckle** is something you use to fasten a belt, a shoe or a bag.
বকলস্

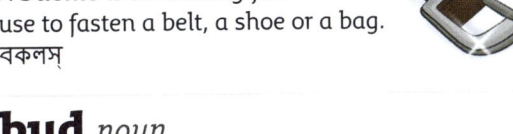

bud noun
buds
A **bud** is a small, new part on a tree or plant that grows into a leaf or a flower.
কুঁড়ি

build verb
builds, building, built
If you **build** something, you make it by putting the parts of it together.
নির্মাণ করা
They are going to **build** the school here.

building noun
buildings
A **building** is a place with walls and a roof.
ভবন
Houses, shops and schools are all **buildings**.

built
⇨ Look at **build**.
We **built** our house on a hill.

bulb noun
bulbs
A **bulb** is the part of a lamp that is made of glass and gives out light.
বাল্ব

bull noun
bulls
A **bull** is a male cow. **Bulls** have horns.
ষাঁড়

bump verb
bumps, bumping, bumped
If you **bump** something, or **bump** into it, you hit it without meaning to.
ধাক্কা
I **bumped** the table with my bag.

bunch noun
bunches
A **bunch** of things is a group of them.
গুচ্ছ
He held a **bunch** of keys.

bundle noun
bundles
A **bundle** is a lot of clothes, sticks or other things that are fastened together.
পুঁটলি

buried
⇨ Look at **bury**.
The pirates **buried** the gold beneath a tree.

burn verb
burns, burning, burned, burnt
1. If you **burn** something, you destroy it or damage it with fire.
জ্বালিয়ে দেওয়া
He **burned** all the rubbish.

2. If you **burn** yourself, you touch something that is hot and get hurt.
পুড়ে যাওয়া
I **burned** myself on the hot iron.

3. If something is **burning**, it is on fire.
জ্বলা
The bonfire is still **burning**.

19

burst - buzz

burst verb
bursts, bursting, burst

When something **bursts**, it breaks open suddenly.
বিস্ফোরিত হওয়া
*The bag **burst** and everything fell out of it.*

bury verb
buries, burying, buried

If you **bury** something, you put it into a hole in the ground and cover it up.
কবর দেওয়া
*Squirrels **bury** nuts to eat in the winter.*

bus noun
buses

A **bus** is a large vehicle that carries lots of people.
বাস
*I go to school on the **bus**.*

bush noun
bushes

A **bush** is a plant with lots of leaves and branches that is smaller than a tree.
ঝাড়

busy adjective
busier, busiest

1 If you are **busy**, you have a lot of things to do.
ব্যস্ত
*We were **busy** cleaning the house.*

2 A **busy** place is full of people.
জনবহুল
*The shops are **busy** today.*

butcher noun
butchers

A **butcher** is a person who sells meat.
কসাই

butter noun

Butter is a soft yellow food that is made from cream. You spread it on bread or cook with it.
মাখন

butterfly noun
butterflies

A **butterfly** is an insect with four large wings.
প্রজাপতি

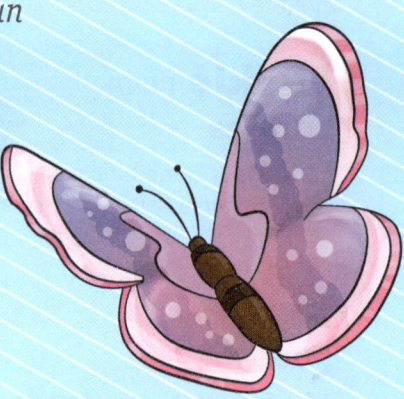

button noun
buttons

Buttons are small, round things on clothes that you push through holes to fasten the clothes together.
বোতাম

buy verb
buys, buying, bought

If you **buy** something, you pay money so that you can have it.
কেনা
*We went into the shop to **buy** sweets.*

buzz verb
buzzes, buzzing, buzzed

If something **buzzes**, it makes a sound like a bee makes when it flies.
গুণগুণ করা
*An insect **buzzed** around my head.*

Cc

cabbage - can

cabbage noun
cabbages
A **cabbage** is a round vegetable with green, white, or purple leaves.
বাঁধাকপি

cage noun
cages
A **cage** is a box or a room made of bars where you keep birds or animals.
খাঁচা

cake noun
cakes
A **cake** is a sweet food made from flour, eggs, sugar, and butter that you bake in an oven.
কেক

calculator noun
calculators
A **calculator** is a small machine that you use to do sums.
যন্ত্রগণক

calendar noun
calendars
A **calendar** is a list of all the days, weeks, and months in a year.
পঞ্জিকা/তারিখ, দিন ও মাস দেখার তালিকা

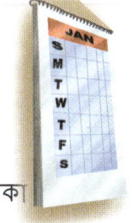

calf noun
calves
1. A **calf** is a young cow.
   বাছুর
2. Your **calves** are also the thick parts at the backs of your legs, between your ankles and your knees.
   পায়ের ডিম

call verb
calls, calling, called
1. If you **call** someone something, you give them a name.
   ডাকা
   *I **called** my cat Pippin.*
2. If you **call** something, you say it in a loud voice.
   চিৎকার করে ডাকা
   *Someone **called** his name.*
3. If you **call** someone, you talk to them on the telephone.
   টেলিফোন করা
   *I'll **call** you tomorrow.*

calves
▷ Look at **calf**.
*My **calves** hurt.*

came
▷ Look at **come**.
*My friends **came** to play at my house.*

camel noun
camels
A **camel** is a large animal with one or two big lumps on its back. **Camels** live in hot, dry places and carry people and things.
উট

camera noun
cameras
A **camera** is a machine that you use to take pictures.
ক্যামেরা

camp noun
camps
A **camp** is a place where people live in tents for a short time.
শিবির

can verb
could
If you **can** do something, you are able to do it.
করতে পারা
*I **can** swim.*

21

can - carry

A B **C** D E F G H I J K L M N O P Q R S T U V W X Y Z

can noun
cans
A **can** is a metal container for food or drink.
কৌটো
She opened a **can** of soup.

candle noun
candles
A **candle** is a stick of wax with a piece of string through the middle that you burn to give you light.
মোমবাতি

cannot verb
If you **cannot** do something, you are not able to do it.
করতে না পারা
I **cannot** find my bag.

can't
Can't is short for **cannot**.
He **can't** play the piano.

capital noun
capitals
1 The **capital** of a country is the main city, where the country's leaders work.
রাজধানী
Paris is the **capital** of France.
2 A **capital** is also a big letter of the alphabet, for example A or R.
বড়হাতের অক্ষর

car noun
cars
A **car** is a vehicle with four wheels and an engine that can carry a small number of people.
মোটরগাড়ী

card noun
cards
1 **Card** is stiff paper.
কার্ড
2 A **card** is a folded piece of stiff paper that has a picture on the front and a message inside. You send **cards** to people at special times, like birthdays.
কার্ড
3 **Cards** are pieces of stiff paper with numbers or pictures on them that you use for playing games.
তাস

cardboard noun
Cardboard is very thick, stiff paper that is used for making boxes.
শক্ত কাগজের বোর্ড

care verb
cares, caring, cared
1 If you **care** about something, you think that it is important.
যত্ন নেওয়া
He doesn't **care** about the way he looks.
2 If you **care** for a person or an animal, you look after them.
দেখা শোনা করা
She **cared** for her pets.

careful adjective
If you are **careful**, you think about what you are doing so that you do not make any mistakes.
সতর্ক
Be **careful** when you cross the road.

careless adjective
If you are **careless**, you do not think about what you are doing, so that you make mistakes.
অসতর্ক
It was **careless** of me to forget my keys.

carpet noun
carpets
A **carpet** is a thick, soft cover for a floor.
কার্পেট

carpet

carrot noun
carrots
A **carrot** is a long, orange vegetable.
গাজর

carry verb
carries, carrying, carried
If you **carry** something, you hold it and take it somewhere with you.
বহন করা
We **carried** our bags to the car.

22

carton noun
cartons

A **carton** is a container made of plastic or cardboard that is used to hold food or drink.
কার্ডবোর্ড/প্লাস্টিকের বাক্স
*I bought a **carton** of milk.*

cartoon noun
cartoons

1 A **cartoon** is a funny drawing.
ব্যঙ্গাত্মক চিত্র

2 A **cartoon** is also a film that uses drawings, not real people or things.
কার্টুন ফিল্ম

case noun
cases

A **case** is a container that is used to hold or carry something.
বাক্স
*He put the camera in its **case**.*

castle noun
castles

A **castle** is a large building with very thick, high walls. Most **castles** were built a long time ago to keep the people inside safe from their enemies.
দুর্গ

cat noun
cats

A **cat** is an animal that is covered with fur and has a long tail. People often keep small **cats** as pets. Large **cats**, for example lions and tigers, are wild.
বিড়াল

catch verb
catches, catching, caught

1 If you **catch** something that is moving, you take hold of it while it is in the air.
লুফে নেওয়া
*I tried to **catch** the ball.*

2 If you **catch** a bus or a train, you get on it.
ধরা
*We **caught** the bus to school.*

3 If you **catch** an illness, you become ill with it.
অসুখে পড়া
*He **caught** measles.*

caterpillar noun
caterpillars

A **caterpillar** is a small animal that looks like a worm with lots of short legs. **Caterpillars** turn into butterflies or moths.
শুঁয়োপোকা

cattle noun

Cattle are cows and bulls.
গবাদি পশু
*There were **cattle** in the field.*

caught
⇨ Look at **catch**.
*I jumped and **caught** the ball.*

cauliflower noun
cauliflowers

A **cauliflower** is a big, round, white vegetable with green leaves.
ফুলকপি

cave noun
caves

A **cave** is a big hole in the side of a hill or a mountain, or beneath the ground.
গুহা

CD noun
CDs

CD is short for compact disc.
সিডি
*I bought the band's new **CD**.*

ceiling - chase

ceiling noun
ceilings

A **ceiling** is the part of a room that is above your head.
ছাদ

centimetre noun
centimetres

A **centimetre** is used for measuring the length of something. There are ten millimetres in a **centimetre**, and one hundred **centimetres** in a metre.
সেন্টিমিটার

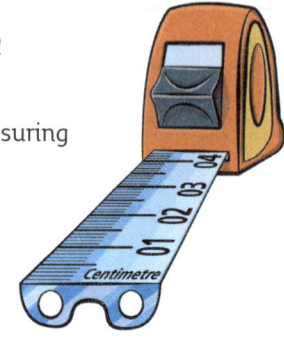

centre noun
centres

The **centre** of something is the middle of it.
কেন্দ্র

*She stood in the **centre** of the room.*

cereal noun
cereals

1 A **cereal** is a food made from grains that you eat with milk for breakfast.
শস্যদানা থেকে তৈরি খাবার

2 A **cereal** is also a kind of plant, for example wheat or rice. The seeds of **cereals** are used for food.
শস্যদানা

chain noun
chains

A **chain** is a row of rings made of metal that are joined together in a line.
শৃঙ্খল

chair noun
chairs

A **chair** is a seat with a back and four legs, for one person.
চেয়ার

*He suddenly got up from his **chair**.*

chalk noun

Chalk is a kind of soft rock. You use small sticks of **chalk** to write or draw on a blackboard.
খড়ি

change verb
changes, changing, changed

1 When you **change** something, or when it **changes**, it becomes different.
বদলানো

*The caterpillar **changed** into a butterfly.*

2 When you **change**, you put on different clothes.
পোষাক পরিবর্তন করা

*He **changed** to go to the party.*

change noun

Change is the money that you get back when you pay too much for something.
টাকা ভাঙ্গান

chapter noun
chapters

A **chapter** is a part of a book.
অধ্যায়

*This book has ten **chapters**.*

character noun
characters

1 Your **character** is the kind of person you are.
চরিত্র

2 A **character** is also a person in a story or a film.
গল্পের অথবা ফিল্মের চরিত্র

charge verb
charges, charging, charged

If someone **charges** you an amount of money for something, they ask you to pay that amount for it.
ব্যয়/মূল্য

*They **charged** us too much for our meal.*

chase verb
chases, chasing, chased

If you **chase** someone, you run after them and try to catch them.
তাড়া করা

*The dog **chased** the cat.*

24

cheap adjective
cheaper, cheapest

If something is **cheap**, you do not have to pay a lot of money for it.
সস্তা

*Milk is very **cheap** in this shop.*

check verb
checks, checking, checked

If you **check** something, you make sure that it is right.
যাচাই করা

*The teacher **checked** my homework.*

cheek noun
cheeks

Your **cheeks** are the sides of your face below your eyes.
গাল

*My **cheeks** were red.*

cheer verb
cheers, cheering, cheered

When people **cheer**, they shout to show that they like something.
আনন্দে চিৎকার করা

*We all **cheered** when he won the race.*

cheerful adjective

Someone who is **cheerful** is happy.
উৎফুল্ল

cheese noun

Cheese is a solid food that is made from milk.
দুগ্ধজাত জিনিস

cheetah noun
cheetahs

A **cheetah** is a big wild cat with yellow fur and black spots.
চিতা

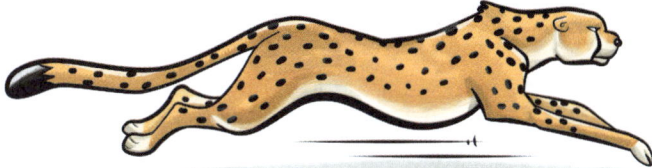

cherry noun
cherries

A **cherry** is a small, round fruit with a hard stone in the middle. **Cherries** are red, black, or yellow.
চেরীফল

chew verb
chews, chewing, chewed

When you **chew** food, you use your teeth to break it up in your mouth before you swallow it.
চিবানো

chick noun
chicks

A **chick** is a very young bird.
মুরগীর বাচ্চা

chicken noun
chickens

1 A **chicken** is a bird that is kept on a farm for its eggs and meat.
মুরগী

2 **Chicken** is also the meat that comes from chickens.
মুরগীর মাংস

child noun
children

A **child** is a young boy or girl.
শিশু

chimney noun
chimneys

A **chimney** is a long pipe above a fire. Smoke from the fire goes up the **chimney** and out of the building.
ধূমনালী/চিমনী

chimpanzee noun
chimpanzees

A **chimpanzee** is a kind of small ape with dark fur.
শিম্পাঞ্জি

chin - class

chin noun
chins
Your **chin** is the part of your face below your mouth.
থুতনি
A black beard covered his **chin**.

chip noun
chips
Chips or potato **chips** are thin pieces of potato fried in hot oil.
আলুভাজা

chip verb
chips, chipping, chipped
If you **chip** something, you break a small piece off it by accident.
টুকরো করা
I **chipped** my tooth when I fell.

chocolate noun
chocolates
Chocolate is a sweet brown food that is used to make sweets, cakes, and drinks.
কোকো বীজের তৈরী

choose verb
chooses, choosing, chose, chosen
If you **choose** something, you decide to have it.
বাছাই করা
You can **choose** any book you want.

chop verb
chops, chopping, chopped
If you **chop** something, you cut it into pieces with a knife or an axe.
টুকরো করা
He **chopped** some wood for the fire.

chose
 Look at **choose**.
She **chose** a dress to wear.

chosen
 Look at **choose**.
We have **chosen** which film to watch.

circle noun
circles
A **circle** is a round shape.
বৃত্ত

circus noun
circuses
A **circus** is a big tent where you go to see clowns and animals.
সার্কাস

city noun
cities
A **city** is a very big town where a lot of people live and work.
শহর

clap verb
claps, clapping, clapped
When you **clap**, you hit your hands together to make a loud noise. People **clap** to show that they like something.
হাততালি দেওয়া
Everyone **clapped** at the end of her song.

class noun
classes
A **class** is a group of people who are taught together.
শ্রেণী
He is in my **class** at school.

classroom noun
classrooms
A **classroom** is a room in a school where children have lessons.
শ্রেণীকক্ষ

claw noun
claws
A bird's or an animal's **claws** are the hard, sharp, curved parts at the end of its feet.
থাবা

clean adjective
cleaner, cleanest
Something that is **clean** does not have any dirt or marks on it.
পরিষ্কার
Make sure your hands are clean.

clean verb
cleans, cleaning, cleaned
When you **clean** something, you take all the dirt off it.
পরিষ্কার করা
I clean my teeth before bedtime.

clear adjective
clearer, clearest
1 If something is **clear**, it is easy to understand, to see, or to hear.
স্পষ্ট
He gave us clear instructions on what to do.

2 If something like glass or plastic is **clear**, you can see through it.
স্বচ্ছ
The bottle was full of a clear liquid.

3 If a place is **clear**, it does not have anything there that you do not want.
ফাঁকা
You can cross the road when it is clear.

clear verb
clears, clearing, cleared
When you **clear** a place, you take away all the things you do not want there.
পরিষ্কার করা
She cleared the table.

classroom - close

clever adjective
cleverer, cleverest
Someone who is **clever** can learn and understand things quickly.
চালাক
She is very clever at maths.

cliff noun
cliffs
A **cliff** is a hill with one side that is very steep. **Cliffs** are often beside the sea.
খাঁড়া উঁচু পাহাড়

climb verb
climbs, climbing, climbed
If you **climb** something, you move towards the top of it. You sometimes use your hands as well as your feet when you **climb**.
আরোহণ করা
We climbed the tree in the garden.

cloak noun
cloaks
A **cloak** is a very loose coat without sleeves.
ঢলঢলে কোট

clock noun
clocks
A **clock** is a machine that shows you the time.
ঘড়ি

close verb
closes, closing, closed
When you **close** something, you shut it.
বন্ধ করা
Please close the door behind you.

27

close - collar

close adjective
closer, closest

If something is **close** to another thing, it is near it.
নিকটে

Our house is close to the park.

cloth noun
cloths

1. **Cloth** is material that is used to make things like clothes and curtains.
   কাপড়

2. A **cloth** is a piece of material that you use to clean something.
   মোছার কাপড়

clothes noun

Clothes are the things that people wear, for example shirts, trousers, and dresses.
জামাকাপড়

cloud noun
clouds

A **cloud** is a white or grey shape that you see in the sky. **Clouds** are made of tiny drops of water that sometimes turn into rain.
মেঘ

clown noun
clowns

A **clown** is a person who wears funny clothes and does silly things to make people laugh.
ভাঁড়

coat noun
coats

You wear a **coat** on top of your other clothes when you go outside.
কোট

cobweb noun
cobwebs

A **cobweb** is a very thin net that a spider makes to catch insects.
মাকড়সার জাল

coconut noun
coconuts

A **coconut** is a very large nut that has a very hard shell and is white inside. **Coconuts** are full of a liquid called **coconut** milk.
নারকেল

coffee noun

Coffee is a drink. You make it by pouring hot water on **coffee** beans.
কফি

Coffee beans grow on a coffee plant.

coin noun
coins

A **coin** is a round, flat piece of metal that is used as money.
মুদ্রা

cold adjective
colder, coldest

1. If you are **cold**, you do not feel comfortable because you are not warm enough.
   শীত লাগা

   Wear a jumper if you are cold.

2. If something is **cold**, it is not hot.
   ঠান্ডা

   The weather is very cold.

cold noun
colds

When you have a **cold**, you sneeze and cough a lot, and you have a sore throat.
সর্দি

collar noun
collars

1. The **collar** of a shirt or jacket is the part that goes around your neck.
   কলার

2. A **collar** is also a band that goes around the neck of a dog or cat.
   গলাবন্ধনী

collect - container

collect *verb*
collects, collecting, collected

1 If you **collect** things, you bring them together.
সংগ্রহ করা
He **collected** wood for the fire.

2 If you **collect** someone from a place, you go there and take them away.
নিয়ে নেওয়া
Mum **collected** us from school.

colour *noun*
colours

Red, blue and yellow are the main **colours**. You can mix them together to make other **colours**.
রং

comb *noun*
combs

A **comb** is a flat piece of metal or plastic with very thin points that you use to make your hair tidy.
চিরুণী

come *verb*
comes, coming, came, come

When you **come** to a place, you move towards it or arrive there.
আসা
She **came** into the room.

comfortable *adjective*

If something is **comfortable**, it makes you feel good.
আরামদায়ক
This is a very **comfortable** chair.

comic *noun*
comics

A **comic** is a magazine with stories that are told in pictures.
ছবিসম্বলিত পুস্তিকা

common *adjective*

If things are **common**, you see lots of them around, or they happen often.
সাধারণ
Foxes are quite **common** in this area.

compact disc *noun*
compact discs

A **compact disc** is a round, flat piece of plastic that has music or information on it. **Compact discs** are also called CDs.
কম্প্যাক্ট ডিস্ক/ সিডি

competition *noun*
competitions

When you are in a **competition**, you try to show that you are the best at something.
প্রতিযোগিতা
She won the painting **competition**.

complete *adjective*

If something is **complete**, none of it is missing.
সম্পূর্ণ
He had a **complete** set of crayons.

computer *noun*
computers

A **computer** is a machine that can store a lot of information and can work things out very quickly.
কম্পিউটার
We played games on our **computer**.

confused *adjective*

If you are **confused**, you do not understand what is happening, or you do not know what to do.
হতবুদ্ধি
She was **confused** about where to go.

consonant *noun*
consonants

A **consonant** is any letter of the alphabet that is not a, e, i, o, or u.
ব্যঞ্জনবর্ণ
The word "book" has two **consonants** in it.

container *noun*
containers

A **container** is something that you use to keep things in, for example a box or a bottle.
পাত্র

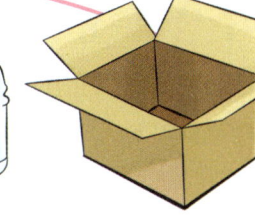

control - couldn't

control verb
controls, controlling, controlled

If you **control** something, you can make it do what you want.
নিয়ন্ত্রণ করা
*I can **control** the speed by pressing this button.*

cook verb
cooks, cooking, cooked

When you **cook** food, you make it hot and get it ready to eat.
রান্না করা
*Mum was **cooking** dinner.*

cooker noun
cookers

A **cooker** is a machine that you use to cook food.
কুকার

cool adjective
cooler, coolest

Something that is **cool** is quite cold.
ঠান্ডা
*Put the milk in the fridge to keep it **cool**.*

copy noun
copies

A **copy** is something that is made to look like another thing.
নকল
*I made a **copy** of the drawing.*

corn noun

Corn is a long vegetable. It is covered with yellow seeds that you eat.
ভুট্টা

corner noun
corners

A **corner** is a place where two sides join together.
কোণ
*He stood at the **corner** of the street.*

correct adjective

If something is **correct**, there are no mistakes in it.
সঠিক

cost noun
costs

The **cost** of something is the amount of money you need to buy it.
দাম
*The **cost** of the holiday was too high.*

cot noun
cots

A **cot** is a bed for a baby, with high sides to stop the baby from falling out.
বাচ্চার খাট

cotton noun

1 **Cotton** is a kind of cloth that is made from the **cotton** plant.
সুতির কাপড়

2 **Cotton** is also thread that you use to sew with.
সুতো

cough verb
coughs, coughing, coughed

When you **cough**, you make air come out of your throat with a sudden, loud noise.
কাশি
*The smoke made us **cough**.*

could verb

If you say you **could** do something, you mean that you were able to do it. **Could** comes from the word **can**.
পারা
*I **could** see through the window.*

couldn't

Couldn't is short for **could not**.
না পারা
*She **couldn't** open the door.*

30

count verb
counts, counting, counted

1 When you **count**, you say numbers in order, one after the other.
পরপর গোনা

I counted from one to ten.

2 When you **count** all the things in a group, you add them up to see how many there are.
গুনে নেওয়া
The teacher counted the children in the class.

country noun
countries

1 A **country** is a part of the world with its own people and laws.
দেশ
He lives in a different country.

2 The **country** is land that is away from towns and cities. There are farms and woods in the **country**.
গ্রামাঞ্চল
We went for a walk in the country.

cousin noun
cousins

Your **cousin** is the son or daughter of your uncle or aunt.
সম্পর্কিত ভাই-বোন

cover verb
covers, covering, covered

If you **cover** something, you put another thing over it.
ঢাকা দেওয়া
She covered the table with a cloth.

cover noun
covers

A **cover** is something that you put over another thing.
ঢাকা
Put a cover over the sofa to keep it clean.

cow noun
cows

A **cow** is a large animal that is kept on farms because it gives milk.
গরু

crab noun
crabs

A **crab** is an animal with a hard shell that lives in the sea. **Crabs** have large claws on their front legs.
কাঁকড়া

crack verb
cracks, cracking, cracked

If something **cracks**, it becomes damaged, and lines appear on the surface where it has broken.
চিড় ধরা
The window cracked.

crane noun
cranes

1 A **crane** is a tall machine that can lift very heavy things.
ক্রেন (যন্ত্র)

2 A **crane** is also a large bird with a long neck and long legs. **Cranes** live near water.
সারস

crash noun
crashes

1 A **crash** is an accident when a vehicle hits something.
গাড়ী দুৰ্ঘটনা
There was a car crash outside the school.

2 A **crash** is also a sudden, loud noise.
আচমকা তীব্র আওয়াজ
He dropped the plates with a crash.

crawl verb
crawls, crawling, crawled

When you **crawl**, you move along on your hands and knees.
হামাগুড়ি দেওয়া
The baby crawled along the floor.

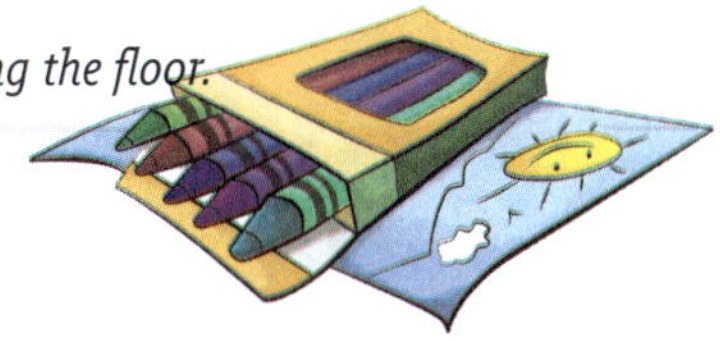

crayon noun
crayons

Crayons are pencils or sticks of wax in different colours that you use for drawing.
মোম-রং

cream noun

Cream is a thick liquid that is made from milk. You can use it in cooking or pour it over puddings.
ননী

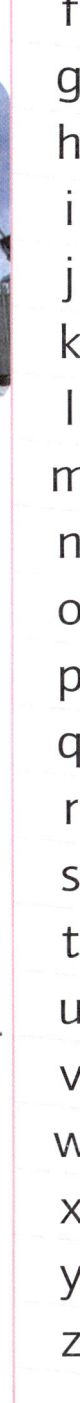

creature noun
creatures

A **creature** is anything that is alive, but is not a plant.
জীব
Many **creatures** live in the forest.

creep verb
creeps, creeping, crept

1 If you **creep** somewhere, you move in a very slow and quiet way.
হামাগুড়ি দেওয়া
He **crept** up the stairs.

2 If an animal **creeps**, it moves along close to the ground.
বুকে হেঁটে চলা
The mouse **crept** across the room.

crew noun
crews

A **crew** is a group of people who work together on a ship or an aeroplane.
বিমান-কর্মীবৃন্দ/জাহাজ-কর্মীবৃন্দ

cricket noun
crickets

1 **Cricket** is a game where two teams take turns to hit a ball with a bat and run up and down.
ক্রিকেট খেলা

2 A **cricket** is also a small jumping insect that rubs its wings together to make a high sound.
ঝিঁঝিঁ পোকা

cried
⇨ Look at **cry**.
The baby **cried** for its mother.

cries
⇨ Look at **cry**.
She always **cries** at sad films.

crocodile noun
crocodiles

A **crocodile** is a large reptile with a long body, a long mouth and sharp teeth. **Crocodiles'** mouths are in the shape of a letter V.
কুমির

crop noun
crops

Crops are plants that people grow for food, for example potatoes and wheat.
ফসল

cross verb
crosses, crossing, crossed

If you **cross** something, you go from one side of it to the other.
পার হওয়া
Cross the road where it is safe.

cross noun
crosses

A **cross** is a mark that you write. It looks like ✕ or ✚.
কাটা চিহ্ন
She put a **cross** beside my name.

cross adjective
crosser, crossest

If you are **cross**, you feel angry about something.
রেগে যাওয়া
Mum was **cross** because we were late.

crowd noun
crowds

A **crowd** is a lot of people together in one place.
লোকের ভিড়
A big **crowd** came to see the game.

crown noun
crowns

A **crown** is a circle made of gold or silver and jewels that kings and queens wear on their heads.
মুকুট

cry verb
cries, crying, cried

When you **cry**, tears come from your eyes. People **cry** when they are sad or hurt.
কাঁদা
The baby started to **cry**.

cry noun
cries
A **cry** is a loud sound that you make with your voice.
চেঁচানো
*I heard the **cry** of a bird.*

cub noun
cubs
A **cub** is a young wild animal, for example a young bear or lion.
সিংহশাবক

cube noun
cubes
A **cube** is a solid shape with six sides that are all squares.
ঘনক
*A dice is in the shape of a **cube**.*

cucumber noun
cucumbers
A **cucumber** is a long, thin, green vegetable that you eat in salads.
শসা

cuddle verb
cuddles, cuddling, cuddled
If you **cuddle** someone, you put your arms around them and hold them close to you.
জড়িয়ে ধরা

cup noun
cups
A **cup** is a small, round container with a handle. You drink things like tea and coffee from a **cup**.
কাপ

cupboard noun
cupboards
A **cupboard** is a piece of furniture with a door and shelves that you keep things in.
দেরাজ
*The **cupboard** was full of toys.*

curl noun
curls
A **curl** is a piece of hair that has a curved shape.
কুন্তল
*The girl had long, black **curls**.*

curtain noun
curtains
A **curtain** is a piece of cloth that you pull across a window to cover it.
পর্দা

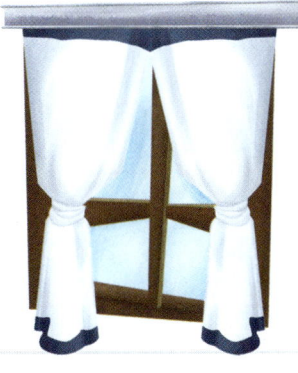

curved adjective
If something is **curved**, it has the shape of a bent line.
বেঁকানো
*The bird had a **curved** beak.*

cushion noun
cushions
A **cushion** is a bag of soft material that you put on a seat to make it more comfortable.
গদিআঁটা

customer noun
customers
A **customer** is a person who buys something in a shop.
ক্রেতা

cut verb
cuts, cutting, cut
1 If you **cut** something, you use a knife or scissors to divide it into pieces.
কাটা
*We **cut** the cake.*

2 If you **cut** yourself, something sharp goes through your skin and blood comes out.
কেটে ফেলা
*Don't **cut** yourself on the broken glass.*

cut noun
cuts
A **cut** is a place on your skin where something sharp has gone through it.
কাটা চিহ্ন
*He had a **cut** on his cheek.*

33

Dd

dad or **daddy** noun
dads or **daddies**

Dad or **daddy** is a name for your father.
বাবা

damage verb
damages, damaging, damaged

If you **damage** something, you break it or spoil it.
নষ্ট করা
*The storm **damaged** the roof.*

damp adjective
damper, dampest

Something that is **damp** is a little bit wet.
আর্দ্র
*Her hair was **damp**.*

dance verb
dances, dancing, danced

When you **dance**, you move your body to music.
নাচা

danger noun
dangers

If there is **danger**, something bad might happen to hurt you.
বিপদ
*There is a **danger** that he will fall.*

dangerous adjective

If something is **dangerous**, it can hurt you or kill you.
বিপজ্জনক
*It is **dangerous** to cross the road here.*

dark adjective
darker, darkest

1 When it is **dark**, there is no light or not much light.
অন্ধকার

2 A **dark** colour is not pale.
গাঢ়
*She wore a **dark** blue skirt.*

date noun
dates

A **date** is the day, the month, and sometimes the year when something happens.
তারিখ
*What **date** is your birthday?*

daughter noun
daughters

Someone's **daughter** is their female child.
কন্যা

day noun
days

1 A **day** is the length of time between one midnight and the next. There are twenty-four hours in a **day**, and seven **days** in a week.
দিন
*It is three **days** until my birthday.*

2 **Day** is the time when there is light outside.
দিনের বেলা
*I've been busy all **day**.*

dead adjective

A person, an animal, or a plant that is **dead** has stopped living.
মৃত

deaf adjective

Someone who is **deaf** cannot hear anything, or cannot hear very well.
কালা

December noun

December is the month after November and before January. It has 31 days.
ডিসেম্বর

decide verb
decides, deciding, decided

When you **decide** to do something, you think about it and then choose to do it.
স্থির করা
She **decided** to go home.

decorate verb
decorates, decorating, decorated

If you **decorate** a room, you put paint or paper on its walls.
সাজানো
We **decorated** the bedroom.

deep adjective
deeper, deepest

If something is **deep**, it goes down a long way.
গভীর
We dug a **deep** hole in the sand.

deer noun
deer

A **deer** is a large animal that lives in forests and can run very fast. Male **deer** have big horns that look like branches on their heads.
হরিণ

defend verb
defends, defending, defended

If you **defend** someone, you keep them safe from danger.
রক্ষা করা
The soldiers **defended** the king.

delicious adjective

If food is **delicious**, it tastes or smells very good.
সুস্বাদু

deliver verb
delivers, delivering, delivered

If you **deliver** something, you take it to someone.
প্রদান করা
Please **deliver** this letter to him.

dentist noun
dentists

A **dentist** is a person whose job is to take care of people's teeth.
দন্ত-চিকিৎসক

depth noun
depths

The **depth** of something is how far down it goes from its top to its bottom.
গভীর
The **depth** of the pond is two metres.

describe verb
describes, describing, described

If you **describe** something, you say what it is like.
বর্ণনা করা
He **described** the picture to me.

desert noun
deserts

A **desert** is a large, dry area of land with almost no trees or plants. **Deserts** are very hot and are often covered with sand.
মরুভূমি

desk noun
desks

A **desk** is a kind of table that you sit at to write or to work.
ডেস্ক

destroy verb
destroys, destroying, destroyed

If you **destroy** something, you damage it so much that it cannot be used any more.
ধ্বংস করে দেওয়া
The fire **destroyed** the house.

diagram - dinner

diagram noun
diagrams

A **diagram** is a drawing that shows something in a way that is very easy to understand.
রেখাচিত্র
He drew me a **diagram** of the engine.

diamond noun
diamonds

1 A **diamond** is a kind of jewel that is hard, clear, and shiny.
হিরে

2 A **diamond** is also a shape with four straight sides.
সমচতুর্ভুজ

diary noun
diaries

A **diary** is a book that you use to write down things that happen to you each day.
দিনপঞ্জী

dice noun
dice

A **dice** is a small cube with a different number of spots on each side. You throw **dice** in some games.
ছক্কা

dictionary noun
dictionaries

A **dictionary** is a book with a list of words in it. The **dictionary** tells you what these words mean, and shows you how to spell them.
অভিধান

did
➪ Look at **do**.
I saw what you **did**.

didn't
Didn't is short for **did not**.
না করা
She **didn't** like the film.

die verb
dies, dying, died

When a person, an animal, or a plant **dies**, they stop living.
মারা যাওয়া
Plants **die** if you don't water them.

different adjective

If two things are **different**, they are not like each other.
আলাদা
The crayons were all in **different** colours.

difficult adjective

If something is **difficult**, it is not easy to do or to understand.
কঠিন
The homework was too **difficult** for us.

dig verb
digs, digging, dug

If you **dig**, you make a hole in the ground.
খোঁড়া
We **dug** a hole in the garden.

digital adjective

If a machine is **digital**, it shows or sends information by using numbers.
অঙ্গুলি সম্বন্ধীয়
We have a new **digital** television.

dinner noun
dinners

Dinner is the main meal of the day.
নৈশভোজ

dinosaur noun
dinosaurs

Dinosaurs were large animals that lived a very long time ago. **Dinosaurs** were like very big lizards.
ডায়নোসর

direction noun
directions

1 A **direction** is the way that you go to get to a place.
দিক
*My house is in this **direction**.*

2 **Directions** are words or pictures that show you how to do something, or how to get somewhere.
নির্দেশ
*He gave me **directions** to the station.*

dirt noun

Dirt is anything that is not clean, for example, dust or mud.
ধুলো
*She had **dirt** on her face.*

dirty adjective
dirtier, dirtiest

If something is **dirty**, it has mud, food, or other marks on it.
ময়লা
*The dishes were **dirty**.*

disappear verb
disappears, disappearing, disappeared

If something **disappears**, you cannot see it any more.
অন্তর্হিত হওয়া
*The cat **disappeared** under the bed.*

disappointed adjective

If you are **disappointed**, you are sad because something you hoped for did not happen.
নিরাশ
*I was **disappointed** that you weren't there.*

disaster noun
disasters

A **disaster** is something very bad that happens suddenly and that may hurt many people.
দুর্যোগ

discover verb
discovers, discovering, discovered

When you **discover** something, you get to know about it for the first time.
আবিষ্কার করা
*We **discovered** that he was very good at football.*

discuss verb
discusses, discussing, discussed

When people **discuss** something, they talk about it together.
আলোচনা করা
*We **discussed** what to do next.*

disease noun
diseases

A **disease** is something that makes you ill.
রোগ
*Measles is a **disease**.*

disguise noun
disguises

A **disguise** is something you wear so that people will not know who you are.
ছদ্মবেশ ধারণ করা

dish noun
dishes

A **dish** is a container that you use to cook or serve food in.
ডিশ

disk noun
disks

A **disk** is a flat piece of metal and plastic that you use in a computer to store information.
ডিস্ক

di**stance** - **do**nkey

distance noun
distances

The **distance** between two things is how much space there is between them.
দূরত্ব
Measure the **distance** between the wall and the table.

dive verb
dives, diving, dived

If you **dive** into water, you jump in so that your arms and your head go in first.
ডুব দেওয়া

divide verb
divides, dividing, divided

1. If you **divide** something, you make it into smaller pieces.
টুকরো করা
Divide the cake into four pieces.

2. When you **divide** numbers, you see how many times one number goes into another number.
ভাগ করা
If you **divide** ten by five, you get two.

do verb
does, doing, did, done

If you **do** something, you spend some time on it or finish it.
করা
I tried to **do** some work.

doctor noun
doctors

A **doctor** is a person whose job is to help people who are ill or hurt to get better.
ডাক্তার

does
⇨ Look at **do**.
She **does** her homework before dinner.

doesn't
Doesn't is short for **does not**.
না করা
He **doesn't** like carrots.

dog noun
dogs

A **dog** is an animal that barks. Some **dogs** do special jobs, like helping blind people.
কুকুর

doing
⇨ Look at **do**.
What are you **doing**?

doll noun
dolls

A **doll** is a toy that looks like a small person or a baby.
পুতুল

dolphin noun
dolphins

A **dolphin** is an animal that lives in the sea and looks like a large fish with a long nose. **Dolphins** are very clever.
ডলফিন

done
⇨ Look at **do**.
She has **done** a drawing.

donkey noun
donkeys

A **donkey** is an animal that looks like a small horse with long ears.
গাধা

don't

Don't is short for **do not**.
না করা
I **don't** feel well.

door noun
doors

You open and close a **door** to get into a building, a room, or a cupboard.
দরজা

double adjective

Double means two times as big, or two times as much.
দ্বিগুণ
His room is **double** the size of mine.

down

When something moves **down**, it goes from a higher place to a lower place.
নিচে
She came **down** the stairs.

drag verb
drags, dragging, dragged

If you **drag** something, you pull it along the ground.
টেনে আনা
He **dragged** his chair to the table.

dragon noun
dragons

In stories, a **dragon** is a monster that has wings and can make fire come out of its mouth.
ড্র্যাগন

drain verb
drains, draining, drained

If you **drain** a liquid, you take it away by making it flow to another place.
নর্দমা দিয়া জল নিকাশ করা
They **drained** the water out of the tunnel.

drank

⇨ Look at **drink**.
She **drank** a bottle of water.

draw verb
draws, drawing, drew, drawn

When you **draw**, you use pens, pencils, or crayons to make a picture.
আঁকা
He likes to **draw** animals.

drawer noun
drawers

A **drawer** is a box that fits inside a piece of furniture. You can pull it out and put things in it.
ড্রয়ার

drawing noun
drawings

A **drawing** is a picture you make with pens, pencils, or crayons.
চিত্র

drawn

⇨ Look at **draw**.
I have **drawn** my house.

dream noun
dreams

A **dream** is something you see and hear in your mind while you are sleeping.
স্বপ্ন
I had a **dream** about winning the prize.

dress noun
dresses

A **dress** is something a girl or a woman can wear. It covers the body and part of the legs.
পোশাক
She wore a yellow **dress**.

dress - dust

dress verb
dresses, dressing, dressed

When you **dress**, you put on clothes.
সাজগোজ করা
He **dressed** quickly because he was late.

drew
➡ Look at **draw**.
She **drew** a picture of a horse.

drink verb
drinks, drinking, drank, drunk

When you **drink**, you swallow liquid.
পান করা
Mum **drinks** a lot of coffee.

drip verb
drips, dripping, dripped

When liquid **drips**, a small amount of it falls from somewhere.
চুঁয়ে পড়া
Water **dripped** from the roof.

drive verb
drives, driving, drove, driven

When someone **drives** a vehicle, they make it go where they want.
চালানো
He knows how to **drive** a car.

drop verb
drops, dropping, dropped

If you **drop** something, you let it fall.
ফেলে দেওয়া
I **dropped** a plate on the floor.

drove
➡ Look at **drive**.
We **drove** to the shops.

drown verb
drowns, drowning, drowned

If someone **drowns**, they die because their face is below water and they cannot breathe.
তলিয়ে যাওয়া

drum noun
drums

A **drum** is an instrument that you hit with sticks or with your hands to make music.
ড্রাম

drunk
➡ Look at **drink**.
Have you **drunk** all the milk?

dry adjective
drier, driest

If something is **dry**, there is no water in it or on it.
শুকনো
My clothes are **dry**.

duck noun
ducks

A **duck** is a bird that lives near water and can swim. **Ducks** have large flat beaks.
পাতিহাঁস

dug
➡ Look at **dig**.
We **dug** a hole in the sand.

dull adjective
duller, dullest

1 Something that is **dull** is not interesting.
    নীরস
    That was a very **dull** book.

2 A **dull** colour is not bright.
    অনুজ্জ্বল
    He wore a **dull** green jacket.

dust noun

Dust is tiny pieces of dry dirt that looks like powder.
ধুলো
The table was covered in **dust**.

40

Ee

each
Each means every one.
প্রত্যেক
*He gave **each** of us a book.*

eagle noun
eagles
An **eagle** is a large bird with a curved beak and sharp claws. **Eagles** eat small animals.
ঈগল পাখি

ear noun
ears
Your **ears** are the two parts of your body that you hear sounds with.
কান
*He whispered something in her **ear**.*

early adjective
earlier, earliest
1 If you are **early**, you arrive before the time that you were expected to come.
তাড়াতাড়ি
*She was too **early** for the party.*

2 **Early** also means near the first part of something.
প্রারম্ভিক
*I got up **early** in the morning.*

earn verb
earns, earning, earned
If you **earn** money, you work to get it.
রোজগার
*He **earned** some money washing the car.*

earth noun
1 The **Earth** is the planet that we live on.
পৃথিবী

2 **Earth** is also the soil that plants grow in.
মৃত্তিকা

earthquake noun
earthquakes
When there is an **earthquake**, the ground shakes and buildings often fall down.
ভূমিকম্প

east noun
The **east** is the direction that is in front of you when you are looking towards the place where the sun rises.
পূর্ব

easy adjective
easier, easiest
If something is **easy**, you can do it or understand it without having to try very much.
সহজ
*These sums are **easy**.*

eat verb
eats, eating, ate, eaten
When you **eat**, you chew and swallow food.
খাওয়া
*She **eats** too many sweets.*

echo noun
echoes
An **echo** is a sound that you hear again because it bounces off something solid and then comes back.
প্রতিধ্বনি
*We heard the **echo** of our voices in the cave.*

edge - enemy

edge noun
edges

The **edge** of something is the part along the end or side of it.
ধার/প্রান্ত
She stood at the **edge** of the pond.

effect noun
effects

An **effect** is something that happens because of another thing.
প্রভাব
The flood was an **effect** of all the rain.

effort noun
efforts

If you make an **effort** to do something, you have to work a lot to do it.
চেষ্টা
She made an **effort** to win the race.

egg noun
eggs

Baby birds, insects, and some other animals live in **eggs** until they are big enough to come out and be born. People often eat hens' **eggs** as food.
ডিম

eight noun
Eight is the number 8.
আট

elbow noun
elbows

Your **elbow** is the part in the middle of your arm where it bends.
কনুই
She put her **elbows** on the table.

electricity noun

Electricity is a kind of energy that is used to make light, to make things hot, and to make machines work.
বিদ্যুৎ শক্তি

elephant noun
elephants

An **elephant** is a very large, grey animal with big ears, a long nose called a trunk, and two long, curved teeth called tusks.
হাতি

eleven noun
Eleven is the number 11.
এগারো

email or e-mail noun

An **email** is a message like a letter that you send from one computer to another.
ই-মেল
I got an **email** from my cousin.

empty adjective
emptier, emptiest

If something is **empty**, there is nothing inside it.
খালি
The bottle was **empty**.

encyclopedia noun
encyclopedias

An **encyclopedia** is a book that gives you information about many different things.
বিশ্বকোষ

end noun
ends

The **end** of something is the last part of it.
সমাপ্তি
He told me the **end** of the story.

enemy noun
enemies

If someone is your **enemy**, they hate you and want to hurt you.
শত্রু

energy noun

1 If you have **energy**, you have the strength to move around a lot and do things.
কর্মশক্তি
*He has the **energy** to run for miles.*

2 **Energy** is also the power that makes machines work.
শক্তি
*The lamp gets its **energy** from the sun.*

engine noun
engines

1 An **engine** is a machine that makes things like cars and planes move.
ইঞ্জিন

2 An **engine** is also the front part of a train that pulls it along.
রেলগাড়ির ইঞ্জিন

enjoy verb
enjoys, enjoying, enjoyed

If you **enjoy** something, you like doing it.
আনন্দ উপভোগ করা
*I **enjoy** reading.*

enormous adjective

Something that is **enormous** is very big.
বিশাল
*Whales are **enormous**.*

enough

If you have **enough** of something, you have as much as you need.
যথেষ্ট
*I don't have **enough** money to buy both books.*

enter verb
enters, entering, entered

When you **enter** a place, you go into it.
প্রবেশ করা

entrance noun
entrances

The **entrance** of a place is the way you get into it.
প্রবেশদ্বার
*We found the **entrance** to the tunnel.*

envelope noun
envelopes

An **envelope** is a paper cover that you put a letter or a card into before you send it to someone.
খাম

environment noun

The **environment** is the land, water, and air around us.
পরিবেশ
*We must try to protect the **environment**.*

equal adjective

If two things are **equal**, they are the same in size, number, or amount.
সমান
*Mix **equal** amounts of milk and water.*

equipment noun

Equipment is all the things that you need to do something.
সরঞ্জাম
*He put his football **equipment** in his bag.*

escape verb
escapes, escaping, escaped

If a person or an animal **escapes**, they get away from somewhere.
পলায়ন করা
*My guinea pig **escaped** from its cage.*

even adjective

1 An **even** number is a number that you can divide by two, with nothing left over.
জোড় সংখ্যা
*Four is an **even** number.*

2 Something that is **even** is flat and smooth.
মসৃণ
*The path was straight and **even**.*

evening noun
evenings

The **evening** is the part of each day between the end of the afternoon and the time when people usually go to bed.
সন্ধ্যাবেলা

ever

Ever means at any time.
কোনদিনও
Have you **ever** seen anything like it?

every adjective

You use **every** to mean all the people or things in a group.
প্রতিটি
Every pupil in the school was there.

everybody

Everybody means all the people in a group, or all the people in the world.
সকলেই
Everybody likes him.

everyone

Everyone means all the people in a group, or all the people in the world.
প্রত্যেকে
Everyone knows who she is.

everything

Everything means all of something.
সবকিছু
He told me **everything** that happened.

everywhere

Everywhere means in every place.
প্রত্যেক স্থানের
I looked **everywhere** for my keys.

example noun
examples

An **example** is something that you use to show what other things in the same group are like.
উদাহরণ
Here is an **example** of my drawings.

excellent adjective

Something that is **excellent** is very good.
অসাধারণ
It was an **excellent** film.

excited adjective

If you are **excited**, you are very happy about something and you keep thinking about it.
উত্তেজিত
He was very **excited** about going to the beach.

excuse noun
excuses

An **excuse** is a reason that you give to explain why you did something.
অজুহাত
She had a good **excuse** for being late.

exercise noun
exercises

1 When you do **exercise**, you move your body so that you can keep healthy and strong.
ব্যায়াম
Running and swimming are both good **exercise**.

2 An **exercise** is also something you do to practise what you have learnt.
অনুশীলন
We did a maths **exercise**.

exit noun
exits

The **exit** of a building is the door you use to get out of it.
বাইরে যাওয়ার রাস্তা
We left by the nearest **exit**.

expect - fair

expect verb
expects, expecting, expected

If you **expect** something to happen, you think that it will happen.
অনুমান করা
I **expect** that he will come.

expensive adjective

If something is **expensive**, you need a lot of money to buy it.
দামী

explain verb
explains, explaining, explained

If you **explain** something, you talk about it so that people can understand it.
ব্যাখ্যা করা
He **explained** to me how the machine worked.

explode verb
explodes, exploding, exploded

If something **explodes**, it bursts with a very loud noise.
বিস্ফোরণ ঘটা

explore verb
explores, exploring, explored

If you **explore** a place, you look around it to see what it is like.
অনুসন্ধান করা
We **explored** the old castle.

extinct adjective

If an animal or a plant is **extinct**, there are none of them alive any more.
লুপ্ত
Dinosaurs are **extinct**.

extra adjective

Extra means more than the usual amount.
অতিরিক্ত
I wore an **extra** jumper because it was cold.

eye noun
eyes

Your **eyes** are the parts of your body that you see with.
চোখ
I opened my **eyes** and looked.

Ff

face noun
faces

Your **face** is the front part of your head.
মুখ
She has a beautiful **face**.

fact noun
facts

A **fact** is something that you know is true.
আসল কথা

factory noun
factories

A **factory** is a large building where people use machines to make things.
কারখানা
He works in a **factory** that makes computers.

fail verb
fails, failing, failed

If you **fail**, you try to do something but you cannot do it.
অকৃতকার্য হওয়া
She **failed** to find her lost keys.

fair adjective
fairer, fairest

1 If something is **fair**, it seems right because it is the same for everyone.
পরিস্কার
It's not **fair** – he's got more than me!

2 **Fair** hair is pale yellow in colour.
ফ্যাকাশে

45

fairy - favourite

fairy noun
fairies

In stories, **fairies** are tiny creatures with wings who can do magic.
পরী

fall verb
falls, falling, fell, fallen

If a person or thing **falls**, they move towards the ground suddenly by accident.
মাটিতে পড়ে যাওয়া
He **fell** off his bike.

fallen
⇨ Look at **fall**.
An apple had **fallen** from the tree.

family noun
families

A **family** is a group of people made up of parents and their children. Aunts and uncles, cousins, grandmothers, and grandfathers are also part of your **family**.
পরিবার

famous adjective

If someone is **famous**, a lot of people know who they are.
বিখ্যাত
She wants to be rich and **famous**.

far
farther, farthest

If something is **far** away, it is a long way away.
দূর
His house was **far** away.

farm noun
farms

A **farm** is a piece of land with buildings on it where people grow crops and keep animals.
খামার

farmer noun
farmers

A **farmer** is a person who grows crops and keeps animals on a farm.
কৃষক

fast adjective
faster, fastest

Something that is **fast** can move quickly.
দ্রুত
This car is very **fast**.

fasten verb
fastens, fastening, fastened

When you **fasten** something, you close it up.
আটকে দেওয়া
She **fastened** the buttons on her coat.

fat adjective
fatter, fattest

Someone who is **fat** has a big, round body.
মোটা

father noun
fathers

A **father** is a man who has a child.
বাবা

fault noun
faults

If something bad is your **fault**, you made it happen.
ত্রুটি
It's my **fault** that we were late.

favourite adjective

Your **favourite** person or thing is the one you like best.
প্রিয়
My **favourite** food is cheese.

fear noun

Fear is the way you feel when you think that something bad is going to happen to you.
ভয়
She shook with **fear**.

feast noun
feasts

A **feast** is a large and special meal for a lot of people.
ভোজ

feather noun
feathers

Feathers are the soft, light things that cover a bird's body. They keep the bird warm and help it to fly.
পালক

February noun

February is the month after January and before March. It usually has 28 days, but once every four years, it has 29 days.
ফেব্রুয়ারী

feed verb
feeds, feeding, fed

If you **feed** a person or an animal, you give them food.
খাওয়ানো
I **feed** my cat twice a day.

feel verb
feels, feeling, felt

1 The way you **feel**, for example happy or sad, or cold or tired, is how you are at the time.
বোধ করা
I **feel** very upset.

2 If you **feel** something, you touch it with your hand to see what it is like.
অনুভব করা
Feel how soft these feathers are.

feet
➡ Look at **foot**.
Don't put your **feet** on the chair.

fell
➡ Look at **fall**.
She **fell** and hurt her knee.

felt
➡ Look at **feel**.
I **felt** angry.

female adjective

A **female** person or animal could become a mother.
নারী

fence noun
fences

A **fence** is a wall made of wood or metal that goes round a piece of land.
বেড়া
There is a **fence** round the garden.

fetch verb
fetches, fetching, fetched

If you **fetch** something, you go to where it is and bring it back.
তুলে আনা
He **fetched** a towel from the bathroom.

fever noun
fevers

If you have a **fever** when you are ill, your body is too hot.
জ্বর

few
fewer, fewest

A **few** means some, but not many.
অল্প কয়েকটি
She gave me a **few** sweets.

field - firework

field noun
fields

A **field** is a piece of land where people grow crops or keep animals.
মাঠ

fierce adjective
fiercer, fiercest

A **fierce** animal is very angry and might attack you.
হিংস্র
That dog looks very **fierce**.

fight verb
fights, fighting, fought

When people **fight**, they try to hurt each other.
লড়াই করা
Two boys started to **fight** in the playground.

fill verb
fills, filling, filled

If you **fill** something, you put so much into it that you cannot get any more in.
ভর্তি করা
She **filled** her cup with tea.

film noun
films

A **film** is a story told in moving pictures that you watch on a screen.
চলচ্চিত্র

fin noun
fins

A **fin** is one of the thin, flat parts on a fish's body that help it to swim.
পাখনা

find verb
finds, finding, found

If you **find** something that has been lost, you see it after you have been looking for it.
খোঁজা
I can't **find** my shoes.

fine adjective
finer, finest

1 If you say that you are **fine**, you mean that you are well or happy.
ভালো
I feel **fine** now.

2 Something that is **fine** is very thin.
মিহি
She sewed the cloth with **fine** thread.

3 When the weather is **fine**, it is dry and sunny.
মনোরম
It is a **fine** day.

finger noun
fingers

Your **fingers** are the long thin parts at the end of each hand.
আঙুল
She put the ring on her **finger**.

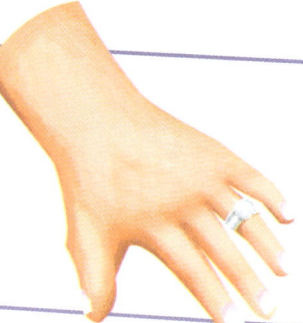

finish verb
finishes, finishing, finished

When you **finish** something, you come to the end of it.
শেষ করা
I **finished** my homework.

fire noun
fires

Fire is the hot, bright flames that come from something that is burning.
আগুন
The **fire** destroyed the forest.

fire engine noun
fire engines

A **fire engine** is a large truck that carries people and equipment to stop fires.
দমকল

firework noun
fireworks

Fireworks are things that make a loud bang or flashes of bright colour when they are burned.
বাজি

firm adjective
firmer, firmest
Something that is **firm** is hard, and is not easy to bend.
শক্ত

first adjective
If a person or thing is **first**, they come before all the others.
প্রথম
January is the **first** month of the year.

fish noun
fish, fishes
A **fish** is an animal that lives in water. **Fish** have fins to help them swim.
মাছ

fit verb
fits, fitting, fitted
If something **fits** you, it is the right size and shape for you.
মাপে হওয়া
These shoes don't **fit** me.

five noun
Five is the number 5.
পাঁচ

fix verb
fixes, fixing, fixed
1. If you **fix** something that is broken, you mend it.
মেরামত করা
He **fixed** the radio.
2. If you **fix** something to another thing, you join them together.
জোড়া লাগানো
She **fixed** the shelf to the wall.

flag noun
flags
A **flag** is a piece of cloth with a pattern on it. Each country of the world has its own **flag**.
পতাকা

flame noun
flames
A **flame** is the hot, bright light that comes from a fire.
অগ্নিশিখা
The **flames** almost burned her fingers.

flash noun
flashes
A **flash** is a sudden bright light.
ঝলক
There was a **flash** of lightning.

flat adjective
flatter, flattest
If something is **flat**, it is smooth and does not have any lumps.
মসৃণ
Lay the painting on a **flat** surface until it is dry.

flavour noun
flavours
The **flavour** of food is the taste that it has.
সুগন্ধ
They had ice cream in lots of **flavours**.

flew
⇨ Look at **fly**.
An aeroplane **flew** across the sky.

flies
⇨ Look at **fly**.
A bird **flies** by moving its wings.

float verb
floats, floating, floated
1. If something **floats** in a liquid, it stays on top of it.
ভাসা
The boat **floated** on the water.
2. If something **floats** in the air, it moves slowly through it.
ওড়া
A balloon **floated** over our heads.

49

flock noun
flocks

A **flock** is the name for a group of birds or sheep.
পাল

flood noun
floods

If there is a **flood**, a lot of water covers land that is usually dry.
বন্যা

We couldn't get to school because of the **flood**.

floor noun
floors

1. A **floor** is the part of a room that you walk on.
মেঝে

There were carpets on the **floor**.

2. A **floor** of a building is all the rooms in it that are at the same height.
তলা

Our house is on the first **floor**.

flour noun

Flour is a powder made from wheat that is used to make bread and cakes.
ময়দা

flow verb
flows, flowing, flowed

If something **flows**, it moves along in a steady way and does not stop.
প্রবাহ

The river **flowed** through the forest.

flower noun
flowers

A **flower** is the part of a plant that makes seeds. **Flowers** often have bright colours and a nice smell.
ফুল

flown
⇨ Look at **fly**.
The birds have all **flown** away.

flu noun

If you have **flu**, you feel as if you have a very bad cold, and your body aches.
ভাইরাসবাহিত রোগ

fly verb
flies, flying, flew, flown

When a bird or aeroplane **flies**, it moves through the air.
ওড়া

fly noun
flies

A **fly** is a small insect with two thin, clear wings.
মাছি

fog noun

Fog is a thick cloud that is close to the ground. It is hard to see through it.
কুয়াশা

fold verb
folds, folding, folded

If you **fold** something, you bend it so that one part of it goes over another.
ভাঁজ করা

He **folded** the letter and put it in the envelope.

follow verb
follows, following, followed

If you **follow** someone, you go along behind them.
অনুসরণ করা

We **followed** him up the stairs.

50

food noun
foods
Food is what people and animals eat.
খাদ্য

foot noun
feet
Your **feet** are the parts of your body that are at the ends of your legs, and that you stand on.
পা

*Stand with one **foot** in front of the other.*

football noun
footballs
1. **Football** is a game played by two teams of eleven people who kick a ball and try to score goals by getting the ball into a net.
ফুটবল খেলা
2. A **football** is the ball that you use to play football.
ফুটবল

forehead noun
foreheads
Your **forehead** is the part of your face that is between your hair and your eyes.
কপাল

*She had a bruise on her **forehead**.*

forest noun
forests
A **forest** is a place where a lot of trees grow close together.
অরণ্য

forever
If something goes on **forever**, it never comes to an end.
চিরদিন

*The film seemed to go on **forever**.*

forgave
➪ Look at **forgive**.
*She **forgave** her brother for spoiling her drawing.*

forget verb
forgets, forgetting, forgot, forgotten
If you **forget** something, you do not remember it.
ভুলে যাওয়া

*Don't **forget** to lock the door.*

forgive verb
forgives, forgiving, forgave, forgiven
If you **forgive** someone who has done something bad, you stop being angry with them.
ক্ষমা করা

*Please **forgive** me for being late.*

forgot
➪ Look at **forget**.
*She **forgot** to bring any money.*

forgotten
➪ Look at **forget**.
*I have **forgotten** my keys.*

fork noun
forks
A **fork** is a tool with three or four thin, sharp points that you use to eat food with.
কাঁটাচামচ

fortnight noun
fortnights
A **fortnight** is two weeks.
একপক্ষকাল

forwards
If you move **forwards**, you move towards the front.
সামনের দিকে

*They ran backwards and **forwards** trying to catch the ball.*

51

fought
➡ Look at **fight**.
The knights **fought** with swords.

found
➡ Look at **find**.
She **found** her lost dog.

four noun
Four is the number 4.
চার

fox noun
foxes
A **fox** is an animal that looks like a dog with red fur and a long, thick tail.
শিয়াল

fraction noun
fractions
A **fraction** is a part of a whole number.
ভগ্নাংশ
A half and a quarter are both **fractions**.

frame noun
frames
A **frame** is a piece of wood, metal or plastic that fits around the edge of a picture, a window, or a door.
কাঠামো

frame

freckles noun
Freckles are light brown spots that some people have on their skin.
ক্ষুদ্র ছাপ/তিল/জড়ুল
His face was covered with **freckles**.

free adjective
freer, freest
1 If something is **free**, you can have it without paying any money for it.
বিনামূল্যে
If you buy a cup of coffee, you get a **free** cake.
2 If you are **free**, you can do what you like or go where you like.
স্বাধীন
You are **free** to come here any time.

freeze verb
freezes, freezing, froze, frozen
1 When water **freezes**, it is so cold that it becomes ice.
জমে যাওয়া
2 If you **freeze** food, you make it very cold so that it will not go bad.
ঠান্ডা করা

fresh adjective
fresher, freshest
1 If food is **fresh**, it has been picked or made a short time ago.
টাটকা
Eat some **fresh** fruit every day.
2 **Fresh** water has no salt in it. The water in rivers is **fresh**.
তাজা
3 **Fresh** air is clean and cool.
তাজা

Friday noun
Fridays
Friday is the day after Thursday and before Saturday.
শুক্রবার
He went home on **Friday**.

fridge noun
fridges
A **fridge** is a cupboard that uses electricity to keep food cold and fresh.
ফ্রিজ
Put the butter in the **fridge**.

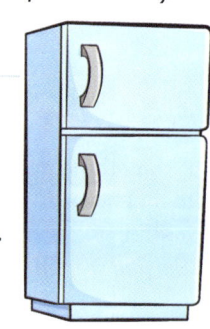

fried
➡ Look at **fry**.
She **fried** some eggs.

friend noun
friends

A **friend** is someone you know and like, and who likes you too.
বন্ধু

friendly adjective
friendlier, friendliest

If someone is **friendly**, they like to meet other people, and are nice to them.
বন্ধুভাবাপন্ন

frighten verb
frightens, frightening, frightened

If something **frightens** you, it makes you feel afraid.
প্রচন্ড ভয় পাওয়া
Loud noises **frighten** her.

frog noun
frogs

A **frog** is a small animal with smooth skin, big eyes, and long back legs that it uses for jumping. **Frogs** live near water.
ব্যাঙ

front noun
fronts

The **front** of something is the part that comes first or the part that you usually see first.
সামনের দিক
She stood at the **front** of the queue.

frost noun

Frost is ice that looks like white powder. It covers things outside when the weather is very cold.
তুষারপাত

frown verb
frowns, frowning, frowned

When you **frown**, lines appear on your forehead because you are cross or because you are thinking about something.
ভুরু কোঁচকানো

froze
➡ Look at **freeze**.
It was so cold that the lake **froze**.

frozen
➡ Look at **freeze**.
The water had **frozen** into ice.

fruit noun
fruits

Fruit is the part of a plant or a tree that has the seeds in it. You can eat many **fruits**, for example apples, bananas, and strawberries.
ফল

fry verb
fries, frying, fried

When you **fry** food, you cook it in hot oil or butter.
ভাজা করা
Fry the onions until they are brown.

full adjective
fuller, fullest

If something is **full**, it has so much in it that it cannot hold any more.
পরিপূর্ণ
The bottle is **full**.

53

fun - garden

fun noun

When you have **fun**, you enjoy doing something and you feel happy.
মজা
*They had **fun** at the beach.*

funny adjective
funnier, funniest

1. If something is **funny**, it makes you laugh.
   মজার
   *He told me a **funny** joke.*

2. **Funny** also means strange.
   আশ্চর্যজনক
   *The car is making a **funny** noise.*

fur noun

Fur is the soft hair that covers the bodies of many animals.
পশুর লোম
*Pandas have black and white **fur**.*

furniture noun

Furniture is the name for all the big things, for example tables, chairs, or beds, that people have in their houses.
আসবাবপত্র
*We bought new **furniture** for the bedroom.*

future noun

The **future** is the time that will come after the present time.
আগামী
*In the **future**, people will travel to other planets.*

Gg

gale noun
gales

A **gale** is a very strong wind.
প্রবল ঝড়

game noun
games

1. A **game** is something you play that has rules, for example football.
   খেলা

2. Children also play a **game** when they pretend to be other people.
   খেলা
   *We played a **game** of pirates.*

gap noun
gaps

A **gap** is a space between two things.
ফাঁক
*There was a **gap** between the curtains.*

garage noun
garages

1. A **garage** is a building where you keep a car.
   গ্যারেজ

2. A **garage** is also a place where you can get your car repaired.
   গাড়ি সারাবার জায়গা

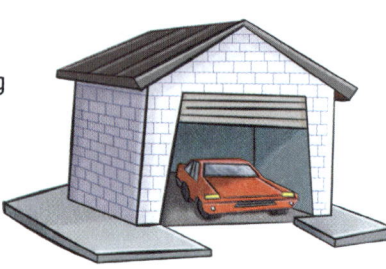

garden noun
gardens

A **garden** is a piece of land near a house where people can grow grass, flowers, and vegetables.
বাগান

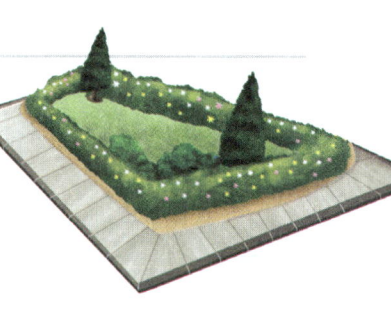

54

gas noun
gases
A **gas** is anything, for example air, that is not solid or a liquid.
গ্যাস

gate noun
gates
A **gate** is a kind of door in a wall, a fence, or a hedge.
দরজা

gave
⇨ Look at **give**.
She **gave** me a present.

gentle adjective
gentler, gentlest
If you are **gentle**, you are careful and not rough.
ভদ্র
Be **gentle** when you hold the baby.

get verb
gets, getting, got
1 You can use **get** to mean the same as "become".
পরিণত হওয়া
We should go before it **gets** dark.
2 If you **get** somewhere, you arrive there.
পৌঁছানো
He **got** home at noon.
3 If you **get** something, someone gives it to you.
পাওয়া
I **got** a bike for my birthday.
4 If you **get** something, you go to where it is and bring it back.
পাওয়া
He went to **get** a cup of coffee.

ghost noun
ghosts
A **ghost** is a dead person who some people think they can see and hear.
ভূত

giant adjective
Something that is **giant** is very large.
বিশাল
They watched the film on a **giant** TV screen.

giraffe noun
giraffes
A **giraffe** is a very tall animal with a long neck, long legs, and dark spots on its body.
জিরাফ

girl noun
girls
A **girl** is a child or a young person who is a female.
মেয়ে

give verb
gives, giving, gave, given
If you **give** someone something, you let them have it to keep.
দেওয়া
We always **give** our mother flowers on her birthday.

glad adjective
gladder, gladdest
If you are **glad**, you are happy about something.
আনন্দিত
I'm **glad** you can come to my party.

glass noun
glasses
1 **Glass** is a hard, clear material that is used to make things like windows and bottles. It is quite easy to break **glass**.
কাঁচ
The salad was in a **glass** bowl.
2 A **glass** is also a container made from glass that you can drink out of.
গ্লাস
He filled his **glass** with milk.

glasses noun
Glasses are two pieces of plastic or glass in a frame that people wear in front of their eyes to help them to see better.
চশমা

55

glove - got

glove noun
gloves

Gloves are things that you wear over your hands to keep them warm. **Gloves** have one part for your thumb and one for all your fingers.
দস্তানা

glue noun
You use **glue** to stick things together.
আঠা

go verb
goes, going, went, gone

1 If you **go** somewhere, you move there from another place.
যাওয়া
Can we go to the park?

2 If you say that something is **going** to happen, you mean that it will happen.
হতে চলেছে
He's going to leave soon.

goal noun
goals

In games like football, the **goal** is the place that you try to get the ball in to, to score a point.
লক্ষ্য

goat noun
goats

A **goat** is an animal about the size of a sheep. **Goats** have horns, and hair on their chin that looks like a beard.
ছাগল

gold noun
Gold is a valuable, yellow metal that is used to make things like rings and necklaces, and also coins.
সোনা

goldfish noun
goldfish

A **goldfish** is a small orange fish that people often keep as a pet.
গোল্ডফিশ

gone
⇨ Look at **go**.
She has gone home.

good adjective
better, best

1 If you say that something is **good**, you like it.
ভাল
That was a good film.

2 If you are **good**, you behave well.
ভাল
Be good while I am out.

3 If you are **good** at something, you do it well.
পটু
She is good at drawing.

goodbye
You say **goodbye** to someone when one of you is going away.
বিদায়-সম্ভাষণ

good night
You say **good night** to someone late in the evening before you go home or go to bed.
শুভরাত্রি

goose noun
geese

A **goose** is a large bird with a long neck that lives near water.
লম্বা গলাওয়ালা হাঁস

gorilla noun
gorillas

A **gorilla** is a large, strong animal with long arms, black fur, and a black face.
গরিলা

got
⇨ Look at **get**.
They soon got tired of the game.

56

grain - ground

grain noun
grains

1 A **grain** is the seed of a cereal plant, for example rice or wheat.
দানাশস্য

2 A **grain** of something, for example sand or salt, is a tiny piece of it.
কণা

gram noun
grams

A **gram** is used for measuring how heavy things are.
ওজন
*There are about 400 **grams** of jam in this jar.*

grandfather noun
grandfathers

Your **grandfather** is your father's father or your mother's father.
ঠাকুর্দা

grandmother noun
grandmothers

Your **grandmother** is your father's mother or your mother's mother.
ঠাকুমা

grape noun
grapes

A **grape** is a small, round, green or purple fruit that grows in bunches.
আঙুর

grapefruit noun
grapefruits

A **grapefruit** is a large, round, yellow fruit with a sour taste.
বাতাবি লেবু

graph noun
graphs

In maths, a **graph** is a picture that uses lines or shapes to show numbers.
গ্রাফ

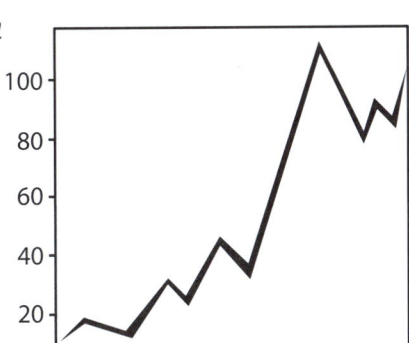

grass noun
grasses

Grass is a green plant with very thin leaves that cover the ground in fields and gardens.
ঘাস

great adjective
greater, greatest

1 **Great** means very large.
বিশাল
*The king lived in a **great** palace.*

2 **Great** also means very important.
মহৎ
*The computer was a **great** invention.*

3 If you say that something is **great**, you mean that it is very good.
সুন্দর
*We had a **great** time.*

greedy adjective
greedier, greediest

If someone is **greedy**, they want to have more of something than they need.
লোভী
*He was so **greedy** that he ate the whole cake.*

green noun

Green is the colour of grass or leaves.
সবুজ
*Her dress is **green**.*

grew

➡ Look at **grow**.
*The tree **grew** to a great height.*

grey noun

Grey is a mixture of black and white, like the colour of clouds when rain is falling.
ধূসর

ground noun

The **ground** is the earth or other surface that you walk on outside.
ভূমি

a b c d e f g h i j k l m n o p q r s t u v w x y z

group noun
groups

A **group** is a number of people or things that are together, or that belong together.
দল

grow verb
grows, growing, grew, grown

When something **grows**, it gets bigger.
বেড়ে ওঠা
The puppy **grew** into a huge dog.

guess verb
guesses, guessing, guessed

If you **guess**, you say what you think is true about something, but you do not really know if you are right.
অনুমান করা
Can you **guess** how old he is?

guinea pig noun
guinea pigs

A **guinea pig** is a small animal with fur and no tail that people often keep as a pet.
গিনিপিগ

guitar noun
guitars

A **guitar** is an instrument with strings that you play by pressing the strings with one hand and pulling them with the other hand.
গিটার

Hh

had
⇨ Look at **have**.
We **had** a nice time.

hadn't
Hadn't is short for **had not**.
ছিল না
I **hadn't** seen them for a long time.

hair noun
Hair is the soft, fine threads that grow on your head and on the bodies of many animals.
চুল
I wash my **hair** every night.

half noun
halves

A **half** is one of two equal parts that make up a whole thing.
অর্ধেক
We each had **half** of the cake.

halves
⇨ Look at **half**.
Cut the apples into **halves**.

hamster noun
hamsters

A **hamster** is a small animal that looks like a fat mouse with a short tail. People often keep **hamsters** as pets.
ধেড়ে ইঁদুরের মত প্রাণী

58

hand noun
hands

Your **hands** are the parts of your body that are at the ends of your arms, and that you use to hold things. A **hand** has four fingers and a thumb.
হাত

*I put my **hand** in my pocket and took out the letter.*

handle noun
handles

1. A **handle** is something that is joined to a door, a window, or a drawer, that you use to open and close it.
   হাতল
   *She pulled the **handle** of the drawer.*

2. A **handle** is also the part of something, for example a tool or a bag, that you use to hold it.
   হাতল
   *Hold the knife by its **handle**.*

hang verb
hangs, hanging, hung

If you **hang** something somewhere, you fix the top of it to something so that it does not touch the ground.
ঝোলানো

*She **hung** her coat on a peg.*

happen verb
happens, happening, happened

When something **happens**, it takes place.
ঘটা

*What's **happening** in the playground?*

happy adjective
happier, happiest

When you are **happy**, you feel pleased about something.
সুখী

hard adjective
harder, hardest

1. Something that is **hard** is solid, and it is not easy to bend it or break it.
   শক্ত
   *The glass broke on the **hard** floor.*

2. If something is **hard**, you have to try a lot to do it or to understand it.
   কঠিন
   *These sums are quite **hard**.*

has
⇨ Look at **have**.
*He **has** a sister.*

hasn't

Hasn't is short for **has not**.
নেই
*She **hasn't** anything to do.*

hat noun
hats

A **hat** is something that you can wear on your head.
টুপি

hatch verb
hatches, hatching, hatched

When a baby bird or other animal **hatches**, it comes out of its egg by breaking the shell. You can also say that the egg **hatches**.
ডিমফুটে বেরিয়ে আসা

hate verb
hates, hating, hated

If you **hate** a person or a thing, you feel that you do not like them at all.
ঘৃণা করা
*I **hate** onions.*

have verb
has, having, had

1. If you **have** something, it belongs to you.
   আছে
   *Do you **have** any pets?*

2. When you **have** something, you feel it, or it happens to you.
   রয়েছে
   *I **have** a bad cold.*

59

haven't - height

haven't
Haven't is short for have not.
নেই
I **haven't** any chocolate left.

hay noun
Hay is dry grass that is used to feed animals.
খড়

head noun
heads

1. Your **head** is the part of your body at the top that has your eyes, ears, nose, mouth, and brain in it.
মাথা
The ball hit him on the **head**.

2. The **head** of something is the person who is its leader.
প্রধান
He is the **head** of the school.

heal verb
heals, healing, healed

If something like a broken bone **heals**, it gets better.
সেরে যাওয়া

healthy adjective
healthier, healthiest

1. Someone who is **healthy** is well and strong and is not often ill.
সুস্থসবল
People need exercise to stay **healthy**.

2. Something that is **healthy** is good for you.
স্বাস্থ্যকর
Eat **healthy** food like fruit and vegetables.

hear verb
hears, hearing, heard

When you **hear** a sound, you notice it through your ears.
শোনা
I **heard** a dog barking.

heart noun
hearts

Your **heart** is the part inside you that makes the blood move around your body.
হৃৎপিণ্ড
His **heart** was going fast.

heavy adjective
heavier, heaviest

Something that is **heavy** weighs a lot.
ভারি
This bag is very **heavy**.

he'd

1. **He'd** is short for **he had**.
ছিল
He'd seen it before.

2. **He'd** is also short for **he would**.
থাকবে
He'd like them.

hedge noun
hedges

A **hedge** is a row of bushes growing close together that makes a kind of wall. You often see **hedges** around fields.
ঝোপঝাড়ের সারি

heel noun
heels

Your **heels** are the parts of your feet at the back, below your ankles.
গোড়ালি
He dragged his **heels** along the ground.

height noun
heights

Your **height** is how tall you are.
উচ্চতা
We all measured our **heights**.

60

held
➡ Look at **hold**.
*Mum **held** my hand as we crossed the road.*

helicopter noun
helicopters
A **helicopter** is a small aircraft with long blades on top that go round very quickly. **Helicopters** can fly straight up and down and stay in one place in the air.
হেলিকপ্টার

he'll
He'll is short for **he will**.
হবে
***He'll** come back soon.*

hello
You say **hello** to someone when you meet them.
শুনছেন !

help verb
helps, helping, helped
If you **help** someone, you make it easier for them to do something.
সাহায্য করা
*He **helped** me with my homework.*

hen noun
hens
A **hen** is a chicken that is a female. People often eat **hens'** eggs as food.
মুরগী

her
You use **her** to talk about a woman or a girl, or to say that something belongs to a woman or a girl.
তার (মহিলা)
*I gave **her** back **her** pen.*

herd noun
herds
A **herd** is a large group of animals that lives together.
পাল
*We saw a **herd** of deer in the forest.*

here
Here means the place where you are.
এখানে
*Come and sit **here**.*

hers
You use **hers** to say that something belongs to a woman or a girl.
তার (নারী)
*She said that the bag was **hers**.*

herself
You use **herself** when you want to say that something a woman or a girl does has an effect on her.
নিজে (নারী)
*She pulled **herself** out of the water.*

he's
He's is short for **he is**.
হল
***He's** six years old.*

hexagon noun
hexagons
A **hexagon** is a shape with six straight sides.
ষড়ভূজ

hid
➡ Look at **hide**.
*They **hid** in the cupboard.*

61

hidden

⇨ Look at **hide**.
He was **hidden** under the bed.

hide verb
hides, hiding, hid, hidden

1 If you **hide** something, you put it where no one can see it or find it.
লুকিয়ে রাখা
He **hid** his bike behind the wall.

2 If you **hide** what you feel, you do not let people know about it.
গোপন করা
She tried to **hide** how angry she was.

high adjective
higher, highest

1 Something that is **high** is tall or is a long way above the ground.
উঁচু
There was a **high** wall around the house.

2 **High** also means great in amount or strength.
উঁচু
They charged us a **high** price.

3 A **high** sound or voice goes up a long way.
উঁচু
She spoke in a **high** voice.

hill noun
hills

A **hill** is a piece of land that is higher than the land around it. **Hills** are not as high as mountains.
ক্ষুদ্র পাহাড়

him

You use **him** to talk about a man or a boy.
তাকে (পুরুষ)
We met **him** at the station.

himself

You use **himself** when you want to say that something a man or a boy does has an effect on him.
নিজে (পুরুষ)
He fell and hurt **himself**.

hippopotamus noun
hippopotamuses or hippopotami

A **hippopotamus** is a large animal with short legs and thick skin that lives near rivers.
জলহস্তী

his

You use **his** to say that something belongs to a man or a boy.
তার (পুরুষ)
He showed me **his** new football.

history noun

History is the story of what has happened in the past.
ইতিহাস

hit verb
hits, hitting, hit

If you **hit** something, you touch it with a lot of strength.
আঘাত করা
She **hit** the ball with the bat.

hive noun
hives

A **hive** is a place where bees live.
মৌচাক

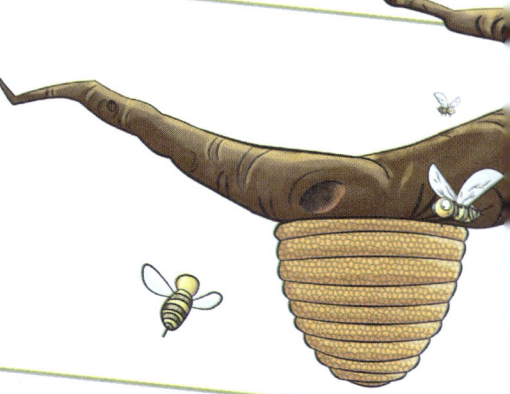

62

hold verb
holds, holding, held

1 When you **hold** something, you have it in your hands or your arms.
ধরা
She **held** the baby in her arms.

2 If something **holds** an amount of something, then that is how much it has room for inside.
ধারণ ক্ষমতা
The theatre **holds** 400 people.

hole noun
holes

A **hole** is a gap or a hollow place in something.
গর্ত
We dug a **hole** in the ground.

holiday noun
holidays

A **holiday** is a time when you do not need to work or go to school.
ছুটির দিন

hollow adjective

Something that is **hollow** has an empty space inside it.
ফাঁপা
The owl's nest was in a **hollow** tree.

home noun
homes

Your **home** is the place where you live.
বাড়ি
We stayed at **home** and watched TV.

homework noun

Homework is something like sums that a teacher gives you to work on at home.
গৃহ কার্য

honest adjective

If someone is **honest**, they do not tell lies, and you can believe what they say.
সৎ

honey noun

Honey is a sweet, very thick liquid that is made by bees. You can eat **honey** on bread.
মধু

hoof noun
hooves

A **hoof** is the hard part of a horse's foot. Deer and cows also have **hooves**.
খুর

hop verb
hops, hopping, hopped

1 If you **hop**, you jump on one foot.
একপায়ে লাফানো

2 When animals or birds **hop**, they jump with two feet together.
দুপায়ে লাফানো

hope verb
hopes, hoping, hoped

If you **hope** that something will happen, you want it to happen.
আশা করা
I **hope** you feel better soon.

horn noun
horns

1 A **horn** is one of the hard bones with sharp points that grow out of some animals' heads. Goats and bulls have **horns**.
শিঙ

2 A **horn** is also an instrument that you blow into to make music.
হর্ন

horrible adjective

If something is **horrible**, it is very nasty.
ভয়ানক
There was a **horrible** smell.

63

horse – hungry

horse noun
horses

A **horse** is a large animal with a long tail and four legs. People ride on **horses** or use them to pull things along.
ঘোড়া

hospital noun
hospitals

A **hospital** is a building where doctors and nurses care for people who are ill or hurt.
হাসপাতাল

hot adjective
hotter, hottest

If something is **hot**, it is very warm.
গরম

*Don't touch the plate – it's **hot**.*

hour noun
hours

An **hour** is used for measuring time. There are sixty minutes in an **hour**, and twenty-four **hours** in a day.
ঘন্টা

house noun
houses

A **house** is a building where people live.
বাড়ি

*Come to my **house** for dinner.*

how
1 You use the word **how** when you ask about the way that something happens or the way that you do something.
কেমন করে

How do you spell your name?

2 You also use **how** when you ask about an amount.
কত

How many people were at the party?

hug verb
hugs, hugging, hugged

When you **hug** someone, you put your arms around them and hold them close to you.
আলিঙ্গন করা

*She **hugged** me as we said goodbye.*

huge adjective

Something that is **huge** is very big.
বিশাল

*Elephants are **huge** animals.*

human adjective

Something that is **human** is to do with people, and not animals or machines.
মানব

*There are over 200 bones in the **human** body.*

hundred noun

A **hundred** is the number 100.
একশো

hung
⇨ Look at **hang**.
*He **hung** from the bars.*

hungry adjective
hungrier, hungriest

If you are **hungry**, you want to eat something.
ক্ষুধার্ত

hunt verb
hunts, hunting, hunted

1. When animals **hunt**, they chase another animal to kill it for food.
   শিকার করা
   The lions **hunted** a zebra.

2. If you **hunt** for something, you try to find it.
   তন্নতন্ন করে খোঁজা
   I **hunted** for my keys.

hurry verb
hurries, hurrying, hurried

If you **hurry**, you move quickly or do something quickly.
তাড়াতাড়ি করা
We'll be late if we don't **hurry**.

hurt verb
hurts, hurting, hurt

If you **hurt** someone or something, you make them feel pain.
দুঃখ দেওয়া
I fell over and **hurt** my leg yesterday.

husband noun
husbands

A woman's **husband** is the man she is married to.
স্বামী

hut noun
huts

A **hut** is a small building with one or two rooms. **Huts** are made of wood, mud, or grass.
কুঁড়েঘর

hutch noun
hutches

A **hutch** is a kind of cage made of wood and wire, where people keep rabbits and other small pets.
খরগোসের খাঁচা

Ii

I

You use **I** to talk about yourself.
আমি
I like chocolate.

ice noun

Ice is water that has frozen. It is very cold and hard.
বরফ
The ground was covered with **ice**.

ice cream noun

Ice cream is a very cold, sweet food that is made from frozen milk or cream.
আইসক্রিম

icicle noun
icicles

An **icicle** is a long piece of ice with a point at the end that hangs down from something. **Icicles** are made from dripping water that has frozen.
তুষার-শলাকা

I'd

1. **I'd** is short for **I had**.
   আমার ছিল
   I'd been there before.

2. **I'd** is also short for **I would**.
   আমার থাকবে
   I'd like to go to the zoo.

idea - information

idea noun
ideas

An **idea** is something new that you have thought of.
ধারণা

He had an **idea** for a story.

ill adjective

When you are **ill**, you do not feel well.
অসুস্থ

She is too **ill** to go to school.

I'll

I'll is short for **I will**.
আমি হব

I'll come back tomorrow.

illness noun
illnesses

If you have an **illness**, you do not feel well.
অসুস্থতা

He has just had a very bad **illness**.

I'm

I'm is short for **I am**.
আমি হলাম

I'm hungry.

imagine verb
imagines, imagining, imagined

If you **imagine** something, you make a picture of it in your mind.
কল্পনা করা

Imagine that you are a cat.

immediately

If you do something **immediately**, you do it now.
অবিলম্বে

Stop that noise **immediately**!

important adjective

1   If something is **important**, people care about it and think about it a lot.
গুরুত্বপূর্ণ

It is **important** not to tell lies.

2   If someone is **important**, people pay a lot of attention to what they say and do.
গণ্যমান্য

She is a very **important** person.

impossible adjective

If something is **impossible**, it cannot be done, or it cannot happen.
অসম্ভব

It is **impossible** to see in the dark.

in

1   **In** means not outside.
ভিতরে

The juice is **in** the fridge.

2   You also use **in** to say when something happens.
এ

He was born **in** March.

inch noun
inches

An **inch** is used for measuring the length of something. There are about two and half centimetres in an **inch**.
ইঞ্চি

indoors

If you are **indoors**, you are inside a building.
গৃহাভ্যন্তর

information noun

Information about something is facts that tell you about it.
তথ্য

I need some **information** about birds.

66

ink - invite

ink noun
Ink is a liquid that you use to write or print with. Pens have **ink** inside them.
কালি

insect noun
insects
An **insect** is a small animal with six legs, for example a bee or a beetle.
Many **insects** have wings and can fly.
পোকা

beetle

inside
1 If something is **inside** another thing, it is in it.
ভেতরে
There was a letter inside the envelope.

2 **Inside** also means indoors.
অভ্যন্তরে
He went inside and locked the door.

instructions noun
Instructions are words or pictures that tell you how to do something.
নির্দেশ
Here are the instructions for building the tent.

instrument noun
instruments
1 An **instrument** is a tool that you use to do something.
যন্ত্র
The doctor used an instrument to look in my ears.

2 An **instrument** is also something, for example a piano or a guitar, that you use to make music.
বাদ্যযন্ত্র
He plays three instruments.

intelligent adjective
If a person is **intelligent**, they are able to understand and learn things quickly.
বুদ্ধিমান

interesting adjective
If something is **interesting**, you want to know more about it.
চিত্তাকর্ষক

Internet noun
The **Internet** is something that joins a computer to other computers all over the world. You send emails using the **Internet**.
ইন্টারনেট

interrupt verb
interrupts, interrupting, interrupted
If you **interrupt** someone, you say or do something that makes them stop in the middle of what they are doing.
বাধা দেওয়া
Don't interrupt the teacher when she's talking.

invention noun
inventions
An **invention** is something that someone has made, and that nobody has ever thought of or made before.
আবিষ্কার
His new invention is a car that can fly.

invisible adjective
If something is **invisible**, you cannot see it.
অদৃশ্য

invite verb
invites, inviting, invited
If you **invite** someone to something, for example a party, you ask them to come to it.
আমন্ত্রণ করা

67

iron - jaw

A B C D E F G H I J K L M N O P Q R S T U V W X Y Z

iron noun
irons

1 **Iron** is a strong, hard, grey metal.
লোহা

2 An **iron** is a piece of equipment with a flat bottom that gets hot. You move the bottom over clothes to make them smooth.
ইস্ত্রী

is
➡ Look at **be**.
She **is** six years old.

island noun
islands

An **island** is a piece of land that has water all around it.
দ্বীপ

isn't
Isn't is short for **is not**.
নয়
He **isn't** very happy.

it
You use **it** to talk about a thing or an animal.
এটি
This is a good book – have you read **it**?

its
You use **its** to say that something belongs to a thing or an animal.
তার
The lion lifted **its** head.

it's
It's is short for **it is**.
এখন
It's one o'clock.

I've
I've is short for **I have**.
আমার আছে
I've been playing football.

Jj

jacket noun
jackets

A **jacket** is a short coat.
জ্যাকেট

jam noun
Jam is a soft, sweet food that is made from fruit and sugar.
জ্যাম
I love strawberry **jam** on my bread.

January noun
January is the month after December and before February. It has 31 days.
জানুয়ারী

jar noun
jars

A **jar** is a glass container with a lid that is used for storing food.
বয়াম
Make sure you put the lid back on the **jar**.

jaw noun
jaws

Your **jaws** are the top and bottom bones of your mouth.
চোয়াল

jaw

68

jeans noun

Jeans are blue trousers with pockets at the front and back.
জিন্স
*Everyone on the trip wore **jeans** and a bright T-shirt.*

jelly noun

Jelly is a clear, sweet food that is solid but soft.
জেলি
*We had birthday cake, then **jelly** and ice cream.*

jet noun
jets

A **jet** is a plane that flies very fast.
জেট

jewel noun
jewels

1 A **jewel** is a valuable stone, like a diamond.
মণি

2 **Jewels** are things made with valuable stones, that you wear to decorate your body.
গয়না
*She put the **jewels** in the box and turned the key.*

jigsaw noun
jigsaws

A **jigsaw** is a picture on cardboard that has been cut up into pieces. You have to fit them together again.
করাত
*The children put the last pieces in the **jigsaw**.*

job noun
jobs

A **job** is the work that a person does to earn money.
কাজ
*My sister wants to get a **job**.*

join verb
joins, joining, joined

1 If you **join** a group of people, you become one of the group.
যোগদান দেওয়া
*Come and **join** the music group after school on Mondays.*

2 When things **join**, or you **join** them, they come together.
যুক্ত করা
*They **joined** hands and danced.*

joke noun
jokes

A **joke** is something that someone says to make you laugh.
কৌতুক করা
*Grandfather always tells us **jokes** after dinner.*

journey noun
journeys

When you make a **journey**, you travel from one place to another.
যাত্রা
*It was a difficult **journey** that took several days.*

jug noun
jugs

A **jug** is a container with a handle. You use a **jug** for pouring liquids.
জগ
*There is a **jug** of cold water on the table.*

juice noun
juices

Juice is the liquid from a fruit or vegetable.
রস
*He had a large glass of fresh orange **juice**.*

July - kept

July noun
July is the month after June and before August. It has 31 days.
জুলাই

jump verb
jumps, jumping, jumped
When you **jump**, you bend your knees and push yourself into the air.
লাফানো
*I **jumped** over the fence.*

jumper noun
jumpers
You wear a **jumper** to keep yourself warm. It has sleeves and covers the top half of your body.
জাম্পার

June noun
June is the month after May and before July. It has 30 days.
জুন

jungle noun
jungles
A **jungle** is a thick, wet forest in a hot country.
জঙ্গল
*They followed the path deep into the **jungle**.*

just
If you **just** did something, you did it a very short time ago.
এইমাত্র
*We **just** got home after an awful journey.*

kangaroo noun
kangaroos
A **kangaroo** is a large Australian animal that carries its babies in a pocket on its stomach.
ক্যাঙ্গারু

keen adjective
keener, keenest
If you are **keen**, you want to do something very much.
আগ্রহী
*Everyone was **keen** to help.*

keep verb
keeps, keeping, kept

1 If someone **keeps** away from a place, they do not go near it.
থাকা
Keep away from the road.

2 If someone **keeps** still or warm, they stay like that.
রাখা
*We lit a fire to **keep** warm.*
*"**Keep** still!"*

3 If you **keep** doing something, you do it many times or you do it some more.
চালিয়ে যাওয়া
*I **keep** forgetting to take my umbrella.*

4 When you **keep** something, you store it somewhere.
রাখা
*She **kept** her money under the bed.*

kennel noun
kennels
A **kennel** is a small house where a dog can sleep.
কুকুরের ঘর

kept
➡ Look at **keep**.
*She **kept** her head down.*

kettle noun
kettles

A **kettle** is a metal container with a lid and a handle, that you use for boiling water.
কেটলি

*Mum put the **kettle** on and made some tea.*

key noun
keys

1 A **key** is a piece of metal that opens or closes a lock.
চাবি
*They put the **key** in the door and it opened.*

2 The **keys** on a computer or instrument are the buttons that you press on it.
বোতাম
*Press the "Enter" **key**.*

kick verb
kicks, kicking, kicked

If you **kick** something, you hit it with your foot.
লাথি মারা
*He **kicked** the ball really hard.*

kid noun
kids

A **kid** is a child.
বাচ্চা
*They have three **kids**.*

kill verb
kills, killing, killed

To **kill** a living thing is to make it die.
মেরে ফেলা
*The earthquake **killed** 62 people.*

kilogram noun
kilograms

A **kilogram** is used for measuring how heavy things are. There are 1,000 grams in a **kilogram**.
কিলোগ্রাম
*The box weighs 4.5 **kilograms**.*

kilometre noun
kilometres

A **kilometre** is used for measuring distance. There are 1,000 metres in a **kilometre**, which is about 0.62 miles.
কিলোমিটার

kind noun
kinds

A **kind** of thing is a type or sort of that thing.
ধরণ
*What **kind** of car is that?*

kind adjective
kinder, kindest

Someone who is **kind** is friendly and helps you.
দয়ালু
*Thank you for being so **kind** to me.*

king noun
kings

A **king** is a man who rules a country.
রাজা
*We saw the **king** and queen arriving.*

kiss verb
kisses, kissing, kissed

If you **kiss** someone, you touch them with your lips.
চুমু খাওয়া
*We **kissed** goodbye at the airport.*

kitchen noun
kitchens

A **kitchen** is a room that is used for cooking.
রান্নাঘর

kite - know

kite noun
kites

A **kite** is a toy that you fly in the wind at the end of a long string.
ঘুড়ি

*We went to the beach to fly **kites**.*

kitten noun
kittens

A **kitten** is a very young cat.
বেড়ালছানা

knee noun
knees

Your **knee** is the part in the middle of your leg where it bends.
হাঁটু

*I fell over and hurt my **knee**.*

kneel verb
kneels, kneeling, knelt

When you **kneel**, you bend your legs and rest on one or both of your knees.
হাঁটু-গাড়া

*She **knelt** down beside the bed.*

knew
⇨ Look at **know**.

*I **knew** all the kids at the party.*

knife noun
knives

A **knife** is a sharp metal tool that you use to cut things.
ছুরি

*I finished and put down my **knife** and fork.*

knight noun
knights

In the past, a **knight** was a soldier who rode a horse.
অশ্বারোহী সৈনিক

knit verb
knits, knitting, knitted

If you **knit** something, you make it from a long piece of wool by using two special sticks.
বোনা

*My grandmother sat **knitting**.*

knives
⇨ Look at **knife**.

*We put all the **knives** away in their box.*

knock verb
knocks, knocking, knocked

If you **knock** on something, you hit it to make a noise.
ঠোকা

*She went to his house and **knocked** on the door.*

knot noun
knots

You make a **knot** when you tie two pieces of something together.
গিঁট

*He picked up the rope and tied a **knot** in it.*

know verb
knows, knowing, knew, known

1 If you **know** something, you have that information in your mind.
জানা

*You should **know** the answer to that question.*

2 If you **know** a person, you have met them and spoken to them.
চেনা

*I didn't **know** any of the other people in the class.*

Ll

label noun
labels
A **label** is a small note on something that gives you information about it.
লেবেল
*The prices are on the **labels**.*

lace noun
laces
1. **Lace** is a pretty cloth that has patterns of holes in it.
লেস
*Her dress was dark blue with a white **lace** collar.*
2. **Laces** are like pieces of string for fastening shoes.
ফিতে
*He put on his shoes and tied the **laces**.*

ladder noun
ladders
A **ladder** is a set of steps that you can move around. You use it for reaching high places.
মই
*He climbed the **ladder** to see over the wall.*

lady noun
ladies
You can use **lady** to talk about a woman in a polite way.
ভদ্রমহিলা
*She's a very nice old **lady**.*

ladybird noun
ladybirds
A **ladybird** is a small round beetle that has red wings with black spots.
এক ধরণের পোকা

laid
⇨ Look at **lay**.
*She **laid** out the food on the table.*

lain
⇨ Look at **lie**.
*He had **lain** awake all night, worrying.*

lake noun
lakes
A **lake** is an area of water with land around it.
ঝিল

lamb noun
lambs
A **lamb** is a young sheep.
ভেড়া

lamp noun
lamps
A **lamp** is a light that uses electricity, oil or gas.
ল্যাম্প
*She turned on the **lamp** by her bed.*

land noun
Land is an area of ground.
জমি
*This is good farm **land**.*

land verb
lands, landing, landed
When something **lands**, it comes down to the ground after moving through the air.
নামা
*The ball **landed** in the middle of the road.*

lane noun
lanes
A **lane** is a narrow road, usually in the country.
গলি

73

language - lead

language noun
languages

A **language** is a set of words that the people of a country use in talking or writing.
ভাষা

The English **language** has over 500,000 words.

lap noun
laps

Your **lap** is the flat area on top of your thighs when you are sitting down.
কোল

The boy sat on his dad's **lap**.

large adjective
larger, largest

A **large** thing or person is big or bigger than usual.
বড়

This fish lives in **large** rivers and lakes.

last adjective
1 The **last** thing is the one before this one.
গত

In the **last** lesson, we looked at some flowers.

2 The **last** thing or person comes after all the others.
শেষ

I read the **last** three pages of the chapter.

late
later, latest

1 **Late** means near the end of a period of time.
শেষবেলা

It was **late** in the afternoon.

2 **Late** also means after the proper time.
দেরি

We arrived **late** for our class.

laugh verb
laughs, laughing, laughed

When you **laugh**, you smile and make a sound because something is funny.
হাসা

The boys all **laughed** at his joke.

law noun
laws

A **law** is a rule that tells people what they may or may not do in a country.
আইন

lawn noun
lawns

A **lawn** is an area of short grass.
লন

Let's sit on the **lawn**.

lay verb
lays, laying, laid

1 When you **lay** something somewhere, you put it down so that it lies there.
শোয়ানো

Lay the dishes on the table.

2 When a bird **lays** an egg, it pushes an egg out of its body.
ডিম পাড়া

lay
➡ Look at **lie**.

We **lay** on the grass and looked at the sky.

layer noun
layers

A **layer** is something that covers a surface, or that lies between two other things.
স্তর

A **layer** of new snow covered the street.

lazy adjective
lazier, laziest

A **lazy** person does not like working.
কুঁড়ে

He was too **lazy** to read the whole book.

lead verb
leads, leading, led

If you **lead** someone to a place, you take them there.
পথ দেখিয়ে নিয়ে যাওয়া

I took his hand and started to **lead** him into the house.

lead noun

If you are in the **lead** in a race or competition, you are winning.
এগিয়ে থাকা
*Our team was in the **lead** after ten minutes.*

lead noun

Lead is a soft, grey, heavy metal.
সীসা

leader noun
leaders

The **leader** of a group of people or a country is the person who is in charge of it.
নেতা
*Your team **leaders** have your instructions.*

leaf noun
leaves

The **leaves** of a plant are the parts that are flat, thin, and usually green.
পাতা
*A dry, brown **leaf** floated on the water.*

lean verb
leans, leaning, leant or leaned

When you **lean**, you bend your body from your waist.
ঝুঁকে থাকা
*She **leant** forwards and looked at me again.*

leap verb
leaps, leaping, leapt or leaped

If you **leap**, you jump a long way or very high.
লাফানো
*He **leaped** in the air and waved his hands.*

learn verb
learns, learning, learnt or learned

When you **learn** something, you get to know it or how to do it.
শেখা
*When did you **learn** to swim?*

leather noun

Leather is the skin of some animals that you can use for making things.
চামড়া
*Is your jacket made of real **leather**?*

leave verb
leaves, leaving, left

1 When you **leave** a place, you go away from it.
প্রস্থান করা
*Our bus **leaves** in an hour.*

2 If you **leave** something somewhere, you do not bring it with you.
ছেড়ে আসা
*I **left** my bags in the car.*

leaves
⇨ Look at **leaf**.
*The **leaves** are beginning to turn brown.*

led
⇨ Look at **lead**.
*The woman **led** me through the door into her office.*

left noun

The **left** is one side of something. For example, on a page, English writing begins on the **left**.
চলে যাওয়া
*The school is on the **left** at the end of the road.*

left
⇨ Look at **leave**.
*The teacher suddenly **left** the room.*

75

leg - lick

leg noun
legs

1. A person's or animal's **legs** are the long parts of their body that they use for walking and standing.
পা
*Stand with your arms stretched out and your **legs** apart.*

2. The **legs** of a table or chair are the long parts that it stands on.
পায়া
*One of the **legs** is loose.*

lemon noun
lemons

A **lemon** is a yellow fruit with very sour juice.
লেবু

lend verb
lends, lending, lent

If you **lend** someone something, you give it to them for a period of time and then they give it back to you.
ধার দেওয়া
*Will you **lend** me your pen?*

length noun
lengths

The **length** of something is how long it is from one end to the other.
দৈর্ঘ্য/লম্বা
*The table is about a metre in **length**.*

lent
➡ Look at **lend**.
*I **lent** her two books to read on holiday.*

leopard noun
leopards

A **leopard** is a large, wild cat. **Leopards** have yellow fur with black spots, and live in Africa and Asia.
চিতাবাঘ

less adjective
Less means a smaller amount.
কম
*I am trying to spend **less** money on sweets.*

lesson noun
lessons

A **lesson** is a period of time when someone teaches you something.
পাঠ
*My sister has a piano **lesson** every Monday.*

let verb
lets, letting, let

1. If you **let** someone do something, you allow them to do it.
হতে দেওয়া

2. You can say **let's** when you want someone to do something with you. **Let's** is short for **let us**.
চলুন
***Let's** go!*

letter noun
letters

1. A **letter** is a message on paper that you post to someone.
চিঠি
*I received a **letter** from a friend.*

2. **Letters** are shapes that you write to make words.
অক্ষর
*The children practised writing the **letters** in class.*

lettuce noun
lettuces

A **lettuce** is a vegetable with large green leaves that you eat in salads.
লেটুস

library noun
libraries

A **library** is a place where you can go to read or borrow books.
গ্রন্থাগার
*I'm going to the **library** to look for a book about whales.*

lick verb
licks, licking, licked

If you **lick** something, you move your tongue over it.
চাটা
***Lick** the stamp before you put it on the envelope.*

lid noun
lids

A **lid** is the top of a container that you can remove.
ঢাকনা
*She lifted the **lid** of the box.*

lie verb
lies, lying, lay, lain

When you **lie** somewhere, your body is flat, and you are not standing or sitting.
শুয়ে পড়া
***Lie** on the bed and close your eyes for a while.*

lie noun
lies

A **lie** is something you say that is not true.
মিথ্যাকথা
*You told me a **lie**!*

life noun
lives

Your **life** is the period of time when you are alive.
জীবন
*I want to live here for the rest of my **life**.*

lift verb
lifts, lifting, lifted

When you **lift** something, you take it and move it up.
ওপরে ওঠানো
*He **lifted** the bag on to his shoulder.*

light noun
lights

1 **Light** is the bright energy that comes from the sun, that lets you see things.
জ্বালান
*A little **light** comes into the room through the thin curtains.*

2 A **light** is something like a lamp, that allows you to see.
বাতি
*There was only one small **light** in the room.*

light adjective
lighter, lightest

1 If a place is **light**, it is bright because of the sun or lamps.
আলোকিত
*It gets **light** at about 6 o' clock here.*

2 Something that is **light** is not heavy.
হাল্কা
*The chair is quite **light** so we can move it if we want to.*

3 A **light** colour is pale.
উজ্জ্বল নয়
*His shirt was **light** blue.*

light verb
lights, lighting, lit

When you **light** a fire, it starts burning.
আলো জ্বালানো
*We used a whole box of matches to **light** the fire.*

lightning noun

Lightning is the very bright flashes of light in the sky in a storm.
বজ্রপাত
*There was thunder and **lightning** and big black clouds in the sky.*

like

1 If things or people are **like** each other, they are almost the same.
ভাল লাগা
*He's very funny, **like** my uncle.*

2 You say what something or someone is **like** when you are talking about how they seem to you.
ধরণ
*"What was the party **like**?"—"Oh it was great!"*

like verb
likes, liking, liked

If you **like** something, you think it is nice or interesting.
পছন্দ করা
*Do you **like** swimming?*

line - load

line noun
lines
A **line** is a long, thin mark or shape.
লাইন
*Draw a **line** at the bottom of the page.*

lion noun
lions
A **lion** is a large wild cat that lives in Africa. **Lions** have yellow fur, and male **lions** have long hair on their head and neck.
সিংহ

lip noun
lips
Your **lips** are the edges of your mouth.
ওষ্ঠ্যযুগল
*He bit his **lip**.*

liquid noun
liquids
A **liquid** is something that you can pour. Water and oil are **liquids**.
তরল
*The bottle is full of clear **liquid**.*

list noun
lists
A **list** is a set of names or other things that you write one below the other.
তালিকা
*There are six names on the **list**.*

listen verb
listens, listening, listened
If you **listen** to something, you hear it and give it your attention.
শোনা
*He's **listening** to the radio.*

lit
⇨ Look at **light**.
*He took a match and **lit** the candle.*

litre noun
litres
A **litre** is used for measuring liquid.
লিটার

litter noun
Litter is rubbish that people drop in the street.
আজেবাজে জিনিষপত্র
*Please don't drop any **litter**.*

little adjective
littler, littlest
A person or thing that is **little** is small in size.
ছোট
*They live in a **little** house.*

live verb
lives, living, lived
1 You **live** in the place where your home is.
বাস করা
*Where do you **live**?*
2 To **live** means to be alive.
বেঁচে থাকা
*We all need water to **live**.*

lives
⇨ Look at **life**.
*Their **lives** were changed.*

lizard noun
lizards
A **lizard** is a small reptile with a long tail and rough skin.
টিকটিকি

load verb
loads, loading, loaded
If you **load** a vehicle, you put something on it.
বোঝাই করা
*We finished **loading** the bags on to the lorry.*

loaf *noun*
loaves

A **loaf** is bread that you cut into slices.
পাউরুটি

*He bought a **loaf** of bread and some cheese.*

lock *verb*
locks, locking, locked

When you **lock** a door, you close it with a key.
তালা দেওয়া

*Are you sure you **locked** the front door?*

log *noun*
logs

A **log** is a thick piece of wood from a tree.
কাঠের গুঁড়ি

*We sat around a **log** fire.*

lolly *noun*
lollies

A **lolly** is a sweet or ice cream on a stick.
এক প্রকারের মিষ্টি

long *adjective*
longer, longest

1 Something that is **long** takes a lot of time.
দীর্ঘ

*The afternoon lessons seemed very **long**.*

2 Something that is **long** measures a great distance from one end to the other.
লম্বা

*There is a **long** table in the middle of the kitchen.*

look *verb*
looks, looking, looked

1 When you **look** at something, you turn your eyes so that you can see it.
দেখা

*I **looked** at the clock and yawned.*

2 You use **look** when you describe how a person seems.
দেখতে

*The little girl **looked** sad.*

loose *adjective*
looser, loosest

1 Something that is **loose** moves when it should not.
আলগা

*One of the table legs is **loose**.*

2 **Loose** clothes are rather large and are not tight.
ঢিলে

*Wear **loose**, comfortable clothes when you do the exercises.*

lorry *noun*
lorries

A **lorry** is a large vehicle for moving things by road.
লরি

lose *verb*
loses, losing, lost

1 If you **lose** a game, you do not win it.
হেরে যাওয়া

*Our team **lost** the match by one point.*

2 If you **lose** something, you do not know where it is.
হারিয়ে ফেলা

*I've **lost** my keys.*

lost *adjective*

If you are **lost**, you do not know where you are.
হারিয়ে যাওয়া

*I suddenly knew that I was **lost**.*

lot *or* lots

A **lot** of something, or **lots** of something, is a large amount of it.
প্রচুর

*He drank **lots** of milk.*

loud *adjective*
louder, loudest

A **loud** noise is a very big sound.
জোরালো

*The music was very **loud**.*

79

love - magnet

love *verb*
loves, loving, loved

1 If you **love** someone, you care very much about them.
ভালোবাসা
2 If you **love** something, you like it very much.
পছন্দ করা
*We both **love** football.*

lovely *adjective*
lovelier, loveliest

A **lovely** thing or person is very beautiful or very nice.
দারুণ সুন্দর
*I thought she looked **lovely**.*

low *adjective*
lower, lowest

1 Something that is **low** is close to the ground.
নীচু
*There is a **low** fence around the house.*
2 A **low** number is a small number.
কম
*The price was very **low**.*

lucky *adjective*
luckier, luckiest

Someone who is **lucky** enjoys good things that people don't expect to happen.
ভাগ্যবান
*He was **lucky** to win the competition.*

lump *noun*
lumps

A **lump** is a solid piece of something.
ডেলা
*There was a bowl full of **lumps** of sugar.*

lunch *noun*
lunches

Lunch is the meal that you have in the middle of the day.
মধ্যাহ্নভোজ

lying
⇨ Look at **lie**.
*There was a man **lying** on the ground.*

Mm

machine *noun*
machines

A **machine** is a piece of equipment that uses electricity or an engine to do something.
যন্ত্র/মেশিন
*I left a message on the answering **machine**.*

made
⇨ Look at **make**.
*Mum **made** me a big birthday cake.*

magazine *noun*
magazines

A **magazine** is a thin book with stories and pictures in it.
ম্যাগাজিন
*I get my favourite **magazine** every Thursday.*

magic *noun*

In stories, **magic** is a special power that allows you to do impossible things.
জাদু
*By **magic**, the man turned to stone.*

magnet *noun*
magnets

A **magnet** is a piece of metal that attracts iron towards it.
চুম্বক

main *adjective*

The **main** thing is the most important one.
মুখ্য/প্রধান
*That's the **main** reason I want it.*

make *verb*
makes, making, made

1. If you **make** something, you put it together or build it from other things.
করা/বলা
*She **makes** all her own clothes.*
2. You can use **make** to show that a person does or says something.
তৈরী করা
*He **made** a phone call.*
3. If you **make** a person do something, they must do it.
বাধ্য করা
*Mum **made** me clean the bathroom.*

male *adjective*

A **male** person or animal could become a father.
পুরুষ
*All of the pupils were **male**.*

mammal *noun*
mammals

Mammals are animals that feed their babies with milk.
স্তন্যপায়ী
*Some **mammals**, like whales, live in the sea.*

man *noun*
men

A **man** is an adult male person.
পুরুষ
*The book is for both **men** and women.*

manage *verb*
manages, managing, managed

If you **manage** something, you control it.
পরিচালনা করা
*He **managed** the bank for 20 years.*

many *adjective*

If there are **many** people or things, there are a lot of them.
অনেক
*Does he have **many** friends?*

map *noun*
maps

A **map** is a drawing of an area from above. It shows where the roads, rivers and railways are.
মানচিত্র
*You can see the park beside this road on the **map**.*

March *noun*

March is the month after February and before April. It has 31 days.
মার্চ মাস

mark *noun*
marks

1. A **mark** is a small dirty area on a surface.
দাগ
*I can't get this **mark** off my shirt.*
2. A **mark** is a shape that you write or draw.
চিহ্ন
*He made a few **marks** with his pen.*

market *noun*
markets

A **market** is a place where people buy and sell things.
বাজার
*There's a **market** in the town centre every Saturday morning.*

marmalade *noun*

Marmalade is jam that is made from oranges.
কমলালেবুর জ্যাম

marry *verb*
marries, marrying, married

When a man and a woman **marry**, they become husband and wife.
বিবাহ করা

mask *noun*
masks

A **mask** is something that you wear over your face to protect or hide it.
মুখোশ

mat - mean

mat noun
mats

A **mat** is a small piece of cloth, wood, or plastic that you put on a table to protect it.
মাদুর
*I put my glass on a red **mat**.*

match noun
matches

1. A **match** is a small, thin stick that makes a flame when you rub it on a rough surface.
প্রতিযোগিতামূলক খেলা
*She lit a **match** and held it up to the candle.*

2. A **match** is a game of football, cricket, or some other sport.
ম্যাচ
*We won all our **matches** last year.*

match verb
matches, matching, matched

If one thing **matches** another, they look good together.
মেলা
*Do these shoes **match** my dress?*

material noun
materials

1. **Material** is cloth.
বস্তু/কাপড়
*Her skirt was made from thick black **material**.*

2. A **material** is what something is made of, like rock, glass or plastic.
উপাদান
*Wax is a soft **material**.*

maths noun

If you learn **maths**, you learn about numbers, shapes, and amounts.
অঙ্ক

matter verb
matters, mattered

If something **matters** to you, it is important.
বিষয়
*Never mind, it doesn't **matter**.*

may verb

1. If you **may** do something, it is possible that you will do it.
হতে পারা
*I **may** come back next year.*

2. If you **may** do something, you can do it because someone allows you to do it.
করতে পারা
*Please **may** I leave the room?*

May noun

May is the month after April and before June. It has 31 days.
মে মাস

me

You use **me** when you are talking about yourself.
আমাকে
*Can you hear **me**?*

meal noun
meals

A **meal** is food that you eat at one time. Breakfast, lunch and dinner are **meals**.
আহার
*She sat next to me for every **meal**.*

mean verb
means, meaning, meant

1. If you ask what something **means**, you want to understand it.
অর্থ
*What does this word **mean**?*

2. If you **mean** what you are saying, it is not a joke.
বলা
*He says he loves her, and I think he **means** it.*

3. If you **mean** to do something, it is not an accident.
মনে করা/চাওয়া
*I didn't **mean** to drop the cup.*

mean adjective
meaner, meanest

Someone who is **mean** is not nice to other people.
নিকৃষ্ট
*He was sorry for being **mean** to her.*

measles noun

Measles is an illness that gives you a fever and red spots on your skin.
হাম

measure verb
measures, measuring, measured

If you **measure** something, you find its size.
পরিমাপ করা
First **measure** the length of the table.

meat noun

Meat is the part of an animal that people cook and eat.
মাংস
I don't eat **meat** or fish.

medicine noun

Medicine is something that you swallow to make you better when you are ill.
ঔষধ
The **medicine** saved his life.

meet verb
meets, meeting, met

If you **meet** someone, you see them and you talk to them.
সাক্ষাৎ করা
I **met** my friends in town today.

melon noun
melons

A **melon** is a large, soft, sweet fruit with a hard green or yellow skin.
তরমুজ
We ate slices of **melon**.

melt verb
melts, melting, melted

When something **melts**, it changes from a solid to a liquid as it becomes warmer.
গলানো
Melt the chocolate in a bowl.

memory noun
memories

1. Your **memory** is the part of your mind that remembers things.
স্মৃতিশক্তি
He has a very good **memory** for numbers.

2. A **memory** is something you remember about the past.
স্মৃতি
They discussed their **memories** of their school days.

men

⇨ Look at **man**.
He ordered his **men** to stop.

mend verb
mends, mending, mended

If you **mend** something that is broken, you repair it.
মেরামত করা
They **mended** the hole in the roof.

mess noun

If something is a **mess**, it is not neat.
বিশৃঙ্খল
After the party, the house was a **mess**.

message noun
messages

A **message** is a piece of information that you send someone.
বার্তা
I got emails and **messages** from friends all over the world.

messy adjective
messier, messiest

A person or thing that is **messy** is not neat.
অগোছালো
His writing is rather **messy**.

met

⇨ Look at **meet**.
We **met** when we were on holiday.

83

metal - mine

metal noun
metals
Metal is a hard material that melts when it gets very hot.
ধাতু
Gold, iron and lead are different kinds of **metal**.

metre noun
metres
A **metre** is used for measuring distances or how long things are.
মিটার
The hole in the ground is about one and a half **metres** across.

mice
⇨ Look at **mouse**.
You can hear the **mice** under the floor.

midday noun
Midday is twelve o'clock in the middle of the day.
মধ্যাহ্ন
At **midday** everyone had lunch.

middle noun
middles
The **middle** of something is the part that is the same distance from each edge or end.
মধ্যে
We stood in the **middle** of the room.

midnight noun
Midnight is twelve o'clock at night.
মধ্যরাত্রি
They went to bed after **midnight**.

might verb
You use **might** when something is possible.
সম্ভাব্য
He **might** win the race.

mile noun
miles
A **mile** is used for measuring distance.
মাইল
They drove 600 **miles** across the desert.

milk noun
Milk is the white liquid that all baby mammals get from their mothers. People also drink **milk** that farmers get from cows.
দুধ
They make cheese from goat's and sheep's **milk** too.

millilitre noun
millilitres
A **millilitre** is used for measuring liquid. There are 1,000 **millilitres** in a litre.
মিলিলিটার
I gave him the medicine with a 5 **millilitre** spoon.

millimetre noun
millimetres
A **millimetre** is used for measuring how long things are. There are 1,000 **millimetres** in a metre.
মিলিমিটার
The small insect was a few **millimetres** long.

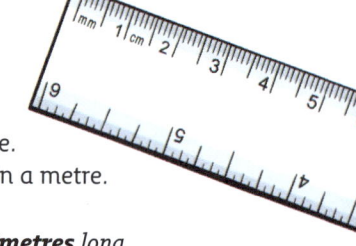

mind noun
minds
Your **mind** is the part of your brain that thinks, understands and remembers.
মন
I can't get that song out of my **mind**.

mind verb
minds, minding, minded
If you **mind** something, it annoys you.
মনে করা
It was hard work but she didn't **mind**.

mine
Mine means belonging to me.
আমার
That isn't your bag, it's **mine**.

mine noun
mines

A **mine** is a deep hole or tunnel where people go to dig things like gold or diamonds out of rock.
খনি

minus

You use **minus** when you take one number away from another number.
বিয়োগ

Three **minus** two is one.

minute noun
minutes

A **minute** is used for measuring time. There are sixty seconds in one **minute**.
মিনিট

The food will take 20 **minutes** to cook.

minute adjective

Something that is **minute** is very small.
অতি ক্ষুদ্র

You only need to use a **minute** amount of glue.

miss verb
misses, missing, missed

1 If you **miss** something that you are trying to hit or catch, you do not manage to hit it or catch it.
ব্যর্থ হওয়া

   I jumped, but **missed** the ball.

2 If you **miss** something, you do not notice it.
লক্ষ্য না করা

   What did he say? I **missed** it.

3 If you **miss** someone who is not with you, you feel sad that they are not there.
অনুপস্থিতি বোধ করা

   The boys **miss** their father.

Miss

You use **Miss** in front of the name of a girl or a woman who is not married when you are talking to her or talking about her.
কুমারী

Do you know **Miss** Smith?

mistake noun
mistakes

A **mistake** is something that is not correct.
ভুল

I made three **mistakes** in my letter.

mix verb
mixes, mixing, mixed

If you **mix** things, you put different things together to make something new.
মেশানো

Mix the sugar with the butter.

mixture noun
mixtures

A **mixture** is what you make when you mix different things together.
মিশ্রণ

The drink is a **mixture** of orange and apple juice.

mobile phone noun
mobile phones

A **mobile phone** is a small phone that you can take everywhere with you.
মোবাইল ফোন

model noun
models

1 A **model** is a small copy of something.
ছাঁচ

   I made the **model** house with paper and glue.

2 A **model** is a person whose job is to wear and show new clothes.
মডেল

   The **model** in the picture was very tall.

mole noun
moles

1 A **mole** is a natural dark spot on your skin.
তিল

   She has a **mole** on the side of her nose.

2 A **mole** is a small animal with black fur that lives under the ground.
ছুঁচো

85

moment - motorbike

moment noun
moments

A **moment** is a very short period of time.
মুহূর্ত
He stopped for a **moment**.

Monday noun
Mondays

Monday is the day after Sunday and before Tuesday.
সোমবার
I went back to school on **Monday**.

money noun

Money is what you use to buy things.
টাকাপয়সা
Cars cost a lot of **money**.

monkey noun
monkeys

A **monkey** is an animal that has a long tail and can climb trees.
বাঁদর

monster noun
monsters

In stories, a **monster** is a big, ugly creature that frightens people.
দানব
The film is about a **monster** in the wardrobe.

month noun
months

A **month** is one part of a year. There are twelve **months** in one year.
মাস
We are going on holiday next **month**.

moon noun
moons

The **moon** shines in the sky at night and moves around the earth every month.
চাঁদ
The first man on the **moon** was Neil Armstrong.

more

You use **more** to talk about a greater amount of something.
বেশি
He has **more** chips than me.

morning noun
mornings

The **morning** is the early part of the day, before lunch.
সকাল
What do you want to do tomorrow **morning**?

most

1 **Most** of a group of things or people means nearly all of them.
বেশিরভাগ
Most of the houses here are very old.

2 The **most** means the largest amount.
সর্বাধিক সর্বাধিক
Who has the **most** money?

moth noun
moths

A **moth** is an insect like a butterfly that usually flies at night.
মথ

mother noun
mothers

A **mother** is a woman who has a child.
মা

motorbike noun
motorbikes

A **motorbike** is a large bike with an engine.
মোটরবাইক

motorway noun
motorways

A **motorway** is a wide road for travelling long distances fast.
দ্রুতগামী গাড়ির জন্য রাস্তা

mountain noun
mountains

A **mountain** is a very high area of land with steep sides.
পর্বত
*Ben Nevis is the highest **mountain** in Scotland.*

mouse noun
mice

1 A **mouse** is a small animal with a long tail.
ইঁদুর

2 You use a **mouse** to move things on a computer screen.
মাউস

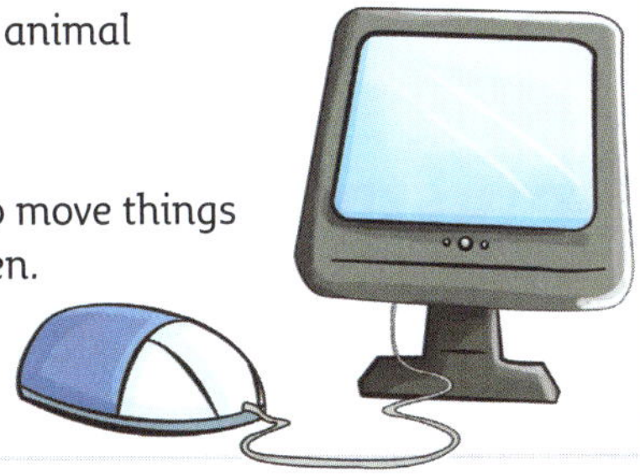

mouth noun
mouths

Your **mouth** is the part of your face that you use for eating or talking.
মুখ
*When you cough, please cover your **mouth**.*

move verb
moves, moving, moved

1 When you **move** something, you put it in a different place.
স্থানান্তরণ
*The man asked her to **move** her car.*

2 If you **move**, you go to live in a different place.
স্থানান্তরে যাওয়া
*She's **moving** to London next month.*

Mr

You use **Mr** before a man's name when you are talking to him or talking about him.
শ্রী
*Our history teacher's name is **Mr** Jones.*

Mrs

You use **Mrs** before a married woman's name when you are talking to her or talking about her.
শ্রীমতী
*How are you, **Mrs** Smith?*

Ms

You use **Ms** before a woman's name when you are talking to her or talking about her.
শ্রীযুক্তা
*The message is for **Ms** Clark.*

much

You use **much** to talk about a large amount of something.
অনেক
*I ate too **much** food.*

mud noun

Mud is a mixture of earth and water.
কাদা
*There was thick **mud** on my football boots.*

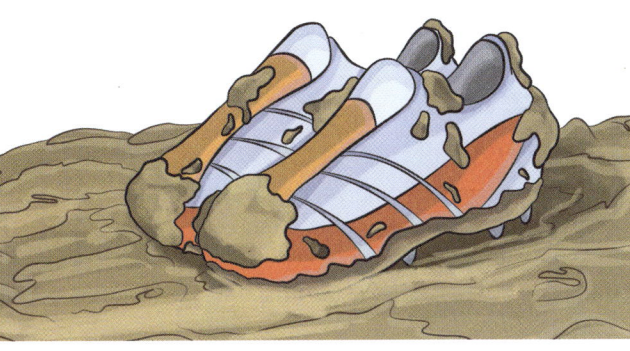

muddy adjective
muddier, muddiest

If something is **muddy**, it is covered with mud.
কর্দমাক্ত
*My boots are all **muddy**!*

mug noun
mugs

A **mug** is a deep cup with straight sides.
মগ
*He poured tea into the **mugs**.*

multiplication – myth

multiplication noun
Multiplication is when you multiply one number by another.
গুণ

multiply verb
multiplies, multiplying, multiplied
If you **multiply** a number, you add it to itself a number of times.
গুণ করা
You get 24 if you **multiply** three by eight.

mum or mummy noun
mums or **mummies**
Mum or **mummy** is a name for your mother.
মা

muscle noun
muscles
Your **muscles** are the parts inside your body that help you move.
পেশী
Sport helps to keep your **muscles** strong.

museum noun
museums
A **museum** is a building where you can look at interesting, old, and valuable things.
যাদুঘর
Hundreds of people came to the **museum** to see the dinosaur bones.

mushroom noun
mushrooms
A **mushroom** is a plant with a short stem and a round top that you can eat.
ছত্রাক
There are many types of wild **mushroom**, and some of them are poisonous.

music noun
Music is the sound that you make when you sing or play instruments.
সংগীত
What's your favourite **music**?

musical instrument noun
musical instruments
A **musical instrument** is an instrument that you use to play music, like a piano or a guitar.
বাদ্যযন্ত্র

must verb
You use **must** to show that you think something is very important.
অবশ্যই
You **must** tell the police all the facts.

mustn't
Mustn't is short for **must not**.
অবশ্যই নয়
I **mustn't** forget to take my key with me.

my
You use **my** to show that something belongs to you.
আমার
I went to sleep in **my** room.

myself
You use **myself** when the you are talking about yourself.
নিজে
I hurt **myself** when I fell down.

mystery noun
mysteries
A **mystery** is something that you do not understand or know about.
রহস্য
Why she's crying is a **mystery**.

myth noun
myths
A **myth** is a very old story about magic, and strange people and creatures.
উপকথা

Nn

nail noun
nails

1 A **nail** is a thin piece of metal. It is flat at one end and it has a point at the other end.
পেরেক
*A picture hung on a **nail** in the wall.*

2 Your **nails** are the thin hard parts that grow at the ends of your fingers and toes.
নখ
*Try to keep your **nails** short.*

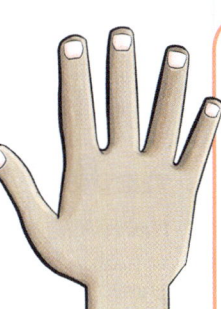

name noun
names

A person's **name** is the word or words that you use to talk to them, or to talk about them.
নাম
*Is your **name** Peter?*

narrow adjective
narrower, narrowest

Something that is **narrow** is a small distance from one side to the other.
সংকীর্ণ
*We walked through the town's **narrow** streets.*

nasty adjective
nastier, nastiest

Something that is **nasty** is horrible.
জঘন্য
*That's a **nasty** thing to say!*

natural adjective

Natural things come from nature.
প্রাকৃতিক
*The **natural** home of these animals is under the ground.*

nature noun

Nature is all the animals, plants, and other things in the world that people did not make or change.
প্রকৃতি
*We watched **nature** all around us from our camp in the forest.*

naughty adjective
naughtier, naughtiest

A **naughty** child does things which are bad.
দুষ্টু
*She was so **naughty**, her mother sent her to bed early.*

near adjective
nearer, nearest

If something is **near** a place, thing, or person, it is not far away from them.
কাছে
*We are very **near** my house.*

nearly

Nearly means almost.
প্রায়
*It's **nearly** five o'clock.*

neat adjective
neater, neatest

A **neat** place or person is clean and tidy.
পরিষ্কার
*She made sure that her room was **neat** before she left.*

neck noun
necks

Your **neck** is the part of your body between your head and the rest of your body.
গলা
*He wore a gold chain around his **neck**.*

89

necklace - newspaper

A B C D E F G H I J K L M **N** O P Q R S T U V W X Y Z

necklace noun
necklaces

A **necklace** is a chain of beads or jewels that you wear around your neck.
নেকলেস
She's wearing a beautiful **necklace**.

need verb
needs, needing, needed

If you **need** something, you believe that you must have it or do it.
প্রয়োজন
I **need** some more money.

needle noun
needles

A **needle** is a small, thin metal tool with a sharp point that you use for sewing.
ছুঁচ
If you get me a **needle** and thread, I'll sew the button on.

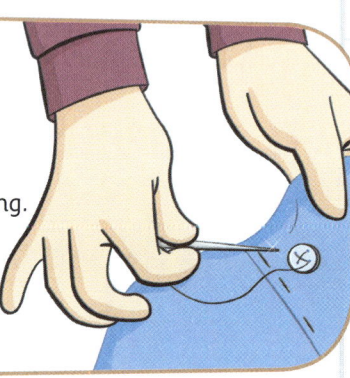

needn't

Needn't is short for **need not**.
প্রয়োজন নেই
You **needn't** come with us if you don't want to.

neighbour noun
neighbours

Your **neighbours** are the people who live around you.
প্রতিবেশী
I met our **neighbour** when I went to the shops.

nephew noun
nephews

Someone's **nephew** is the son of their sister or brother.
ভাগ্নে/ভাইপো
I have a **nephew** who is still a baby.

nervous adjective

If you are **nervous** about something, it worries you and you are rather afraid.
বিচলিত
I tried not to show that I was **nervous**.

nest noun
nests

A **nest** is the place where a bird keeps its eggs or its babies.
বাসা
There were six small eggs in the bird's **nest**.

net noun
nets

A **net** is made from pieces of string or rope tied together with holes between them. It is for catching things like fish, or the ball in some sports.
জাল
The idea is to throw the ball into the top of the **net**.

never

Never means at no time in the past, present or future.
কখনও নয়
Never look straight at the sun.

new adjective
newer, newest

1 Something that is **new** was not there before.
নতুন
They discovered a **new** medicine for his illness.

2 If something is **new**, nobody has used it before.
নতুন
I am wearing my **new** shoes.

3 A **new** thing or person is a different one from the one you had before.
নতুন
We have a **new** history teacher.

news noun

News is information that you did not know before.
খবর
We waited and waited for **news** of him.

newspaper noun
newspapers

A **newspaper** is a number of large sheets of paper with news and other information printed on them.
সংবাদপত্র
They read about it in the **newspaper**.

next *adjective*

The **next** thing is the one that comes immediately after this one or after the last one.
পরবর্তী
*I got up early the **next** morning.*

nice *adjective*
nicer, nicest

If something is **nice**, you like it.
সুন্দর
*They live in a really **nice** house.*

niece *noun*
nieces

Someone's **niece** is the daughter of their sister or brother.
ভাইঝি/ভাগ্নী
*He bought a present for his **niece**.*

night *noun*
nights

The **night** is the time when it is dark outside, and most people sleep.
রাত
*It's eleven o'clock at **night** in Beijing.*

nightdress *noun*
nightdresses

A **nightdress** is a loose dress that a woman or girl can wear to sleep in.
রাতপোষাক

nightmare *noun*
nightmares

A **nightmare** is a dream that frightens or worries you.
দুঃস্বপ্ন
*She had a **nightmare** last night.*

nine

Nine is the number 9.
নয়

no

You use **no** to say that something is not true or to refuse something.
না
*"Would you like a drink?"—"**No** thank you."*

nobody *noun*

Nobody means not one person.
কোন ব্যক্তি নয়
*For a long time, **nobody** spoke.*

nod *verb*
nods, nodding, nodded

When you **nod**, you move your head up and down, usually to show that you agree.
মাথা নেড়ে সম্মতি জানানো
*She **nodded** and smiled.*

noise *noun*
noises

A **noise** is a loud sound.
কোলাহল
*Suddenly there was a **noise** like thunder.*

noisy *adjective*
noisier, noisiest

A **noisy** person or thing makes a lot of loud noise.
কোলাহলপূর্ণ
*It was a very **noisy** party.*

none

None means not one or not any.
কেউ নয়
***None** of us knew her.*

nonsense *noun*

If something is **nonsense**, it is not true or it is silly.
বোকাবোকা
*My father said the story was **nonsense**.*

noon *noun*

Noon is twelve o'clock in the middle of the day.
দ্বিপ্রহর
*The lesson started at **noon**.*

north - nut

north noun
The **north** is the direction to your left when you are looking towards the place where the sun rises.
উত্তর দিক

nose noun
noses
Your **nose** is the part of your face above your mouth that you use for breathing and for noticing smells.
নাক

*She sneezed and blew her **nose**.*

nostril noun
nostrils
Your **nostrils** are the two holes at the end of your nose.
নাসারন্ধ্র

*Keeping your mouth closed, breathe in through your **nostrils**.*

note noun
notes
1 A **note** is a short letter or message.
স্মারকলিপি

*He wrote her a **note** and left it on the table.*

2 A **note** is one musical sound.
ধ্বনি

*She played some **notes** on her recorder.*

nothing
Nothing means not anything.
কিছু না

*There was **nothing** to do.*

notice verb
notices, noticing, noticed
If you **notice** something, you suddenly see or hear it.
দেখতে পাওয়া

*Did you **notice** him leave the room?*

notice noun
notices
A **notice** is a sign that gives information or instructions.
সূচনা

*The **notice** said "Please close the door."*

noun noun
nouns
A **noun** is a word that is used for talking about a person or thing. Examples of **nouns** are "child", "table", "sun", and "strength".
বিশেষ্য পদ

November noun
November is the month after October and before December. It has 30 days.
নভেম্বর

now
You use **now** to talk about the present time.
এখন

*I must go **now**.*

nowhere
Nowhere means not anywhere.
কোথাও না

*There's **nowhere** quiet for me to do my homework.*

number noun
numbers
A **number** is a word that you use to count.
সংখ্যা

*What **number** is your house?*

nurse noun
nurses
A **nurse** is a person whose job is to care for people who are ill.
সেবিকা

*She thanked the **nurses** at the hospital.*

nut noun
nuts
A **nut** is a dry fruit with a hard shell.
বাদাম

***Nuts** and seeds are very good for you.*

Oo

oak noun
oaks
An **oak** tree is a big, tall tree with a wide trunk. Its wood is good for making furniture.
ওক

oar noun
oars
An **oar** is a long piece of wood with a wide, flat end, used for moving a boat through the water.
বৈঠা/দাঁড়

obey verb
obeys, obeying, obeyed
If you **obey** a person or an order, you do what you are told to do.
মান্য করা

ocean noun
oceans
An **ocean** is a big sea.
মহাসমুদ্র
We crossed the Atlantic **Ocean**.

o'clock noun
You say **o'clock** when saying what time it is.
টা বাজছে
It is eight **o'clock** in the morning.

octagon noun
octagons
An **octagon** is a shape with eight straight sides.
অষ্টভুজ

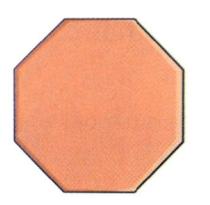

October noun
October is the month after September and before November. It has 31 days.
অক্টোবর

octopus noun
octopuses
An **octopus** is a soft ocean animal with eight long arms.
অক্টোপাস

odd adjective
odder, oddest
1. If something is **odd**, it is strange or unusual.
বিষম
There was an **odd** smell in the kitchen.
2. You say that two things are **odd** when they do not belong to the same set or pair.
বিজোড়
I'm wearing **odd** socks.
3. **Odd** numbers, such as 3 and 17, are numbers that cannot be divided by the number two.
বিজোড়

off
1. If you take something **off** another thing, it is no longer on it.
বিচ্ছিন্ন করা
He took his feet **off** the desk.
2. When something that uses electricity is **off**, it is not using electricity.
বন্ধ করা
The light was **off**.

offer verb
offers, offering, offered
If you **offer** something to someone, you ask them if they would like to have it.
প্রস্তাব দেওয়া
He **offered** his seat to the young woman.

93

office - orchestra

office noun
offices

An **office** is a room where people work at desks.
কার্যস্থান/অফিস

often
Something that happens **often** happens many times or a lot of the time.
প্রায়ই

oil noun
Oil is a thick liquid.
তেল
We need some cooking oil.

old adjective
older, oldest

1 An **old** person is someone who has lived for a long time.
বয়োবৃদ্ধ
An old lady sat next to me.

2 An **old** thing is something that somebody made a long time ago.
পুরানো
We have a very old car.

on

1 If someone or something is **on** a surface, it is resting there.
ওপরে
There was a large box on the table.

2 When something that uses electricity is **on**, it is using electricity.
চালু
The television is on.

once
If something happens **once**, it happens one time only.
একবার
I met her once, at a party.

one noun
One is the number 1.
এক

onion noun
onions

An **onion** is a small, round vegetable with a brown skin like paper and a very strong taste.
পিঁয়াজ

only

1 If you talk about the **only** thing or person, you mean that there are no others.
মাত্র
It was the only shop in the town.

2 You use **only** when you are saying how small or short something is.
কেবলমাত্র
Their house is only a few miles from here.

3 If you are an **only** child, you have no brothers or sisters.
একমাত্র

open verb
opens, opening, opened

1 When you **open** something, or when it **opens**, you move it so that it is no longer closed.
উন্মুক্ত করা
She opened the door.

2 When a shop or office **opens**, people are able to go in.
খোলা
The banks will open again on Monday morning.

opposite

1 If one thing is **opposite** another, it is across from it.
সামনাসামনি
Jennie sat opposite Sam at breakfast.

2 If things are **opposite**, they are as different as they can be.
বিপরীত
We watched the cars driving in the opposite direction.

orange noun

1 An **orange** is a round fruit with a thick skin and lots of juice.
কমলালেবু

2 **Orange** is a colour between red and yellow.
কমলারঙ
Tigers are orange with black stripes.

orchestra noun
orchestras

An **orchestra** is a large group of people who play music together.
অর্কেস্ট্রা
The orchestra began to play.

order verb
orders, ordering, ordered

If you **order** someone to do something, you tell them to do it.
আদেশ দেওয়া
She **ordered** him to leave.

ordinary adjective

Ordinary means not special or different in any way.
সাধারণ
It was just an **ordinary** day.

other adjective
others

Other people or things are different people or things.
অন্যান্য
All the **other** children had gone home.

our

You use **our** to show that something belongs to you and one or more other people.
আমাদের
Our house is near the school.

ours

You use **ours** when you are talking about something that belongs to you and one or more other people.
আমাদের
That car is **ours**.

out

1   If you go **out** of a place, you leave it.
    বাইরে বেরিয়ে আসা
    She ran **out** of the house.

2   If you are **out**, you are not at home.
    বাইরে
    I called you yesterday, but you were **out**.

3   If a light is **out**, it is no longer shining.
    চলে যাওয়া
    All the lights were **out** in the house.

outside

1   The **outside** of something is the part that covers the rest of it.
    বাইরের দিক
    They are painting the **outside** of the building.

2   If you are **outside**, you are not in a building.
    বাইরে
    Let's play **outside**.

oval adjective

Oval things have a shape like an egg.
ডিম্বাকৃতি
She has an **oval** table.

oven noun
ovens

An **oven** is the part of a cooker like a large metal box with a door.
পাউরুটির চুল্লী

over

1   If one thing is **over** another thing, the first thing is above or higher than the second thing.
    ওপরে
    There was a lamp **over** the table.

2   If something is **over**, it has finished.
    শেষ
    The class is **over**.

owe verb
owes, owing, owed

If you **owe** money to someone, you have to pay money to them.
ঋণী থাকা
He **owes** him $50.

owl noun
owls

An **owl** is a bird with large eyes that hunts at night.
পেঁচা

own

You use **own** to say that something belongs to you.
নিজের
Jennifer wanted her **own** room.

ox noun
oxen

An **ox** is a kind of bull that is used for carrying or pulling things.
ষাঁড়

95

Pp

pack verb
packs, packing, packed

When you **pack** a bag, you put clothes and other things into it, because you are going away.
গোছানো

paddle noun
paddles

A **paddle** is a short oar. You use it to move a small boat through water.
ক্ষেপণী সঞ্চালনে অগ্রসর করা/দাঁড় বাহিয়া যাওয়া

paddle verb
paddles, paddling, paddled

1 If someone **paddles** a boat, they move it using a paddle.
দাঁড় চালানো
2 If you **paddle**, you walk in shallow water.
অগভীর জলে চলা

page noun
pages

A **page** is one side of a piece of paper in a book, a magazine, or a newspaper.
পৃষ্ঠা
Turn to **page** 4.

paid
➡ Look at **pay**.
Daddy **paid** for the sweets.

pain noun
pains

Pain is the feeling that you have in a part of your body, because of illness or an accident.
বেদনা
I felt a sudden sharp **pain** in my ankle.

painful adjective

If a part of your body is **painful**, it hurts.
বেদনাদায়ক
His right knee is very **painful**.

paint noun
paints

Paint is a liquid used to decorate buildings, or to make a picture.
রঙ
Can I use some of your red **paint**?

paint verb
paints, painting, painted

1 If you **paint** something on a piece of paper or cloth, you make a picture of it using paint.
রঙ করা
He likes **painting** flowers.
2 If you **paint** a wall or a door, you cover it with paint.
রঙ করা

painting noun
paintings

A **painting** is a picture made with paint.
চিত্র
He's doing a **painting** of a bowl of fruit.

pair noun
pairs

A **pair** of things is two things of the same size and shape that are used together.
জোড়া
She wore a **pair** of plain black shoes.

palace noun
palaces

A **palace** is a very large house where important people live.
প্রাসাদ

pale adjective
paler, palest

A **pale** colour is not strong or bright.
ফ্যাকাসে
She's wearing a **pale** blue dress.

96

palm noun
palms

1. A **palm** or a **palm tree** is a tree that grows in hot countries. It has long leaves at the top, and no branches.
   তালগাছ

2. The **palm** of your hand is the inside part of your hand, between your fingers and your wrist.
   হাতের তালু

panda noun
pandas

A **panda** is a large animal with black and white fur.
পান্ডা

pantomime noun
pantomimes

A **pantomime** is a play that has a funny story with music and songs.
কেবল অঙ্গভঙ্গীদ্বারা অভিনয়

paper noun
papers

1. **Paper** is a material that you write on or wrap things with.
   কাগজ

   He wrote his name down on a piece of **paper**.

2. A **paper** is a newspaper.
   খবরের কাগজ

parcel noun
parcels

A **parcel** is something that is wrapped in paper.
মোড়ক

parent noun
parents

Your **parents** are your mother and father.
পিতা বা মাতা

park noun
parks

A **park** is a place with grass and trees. People go to **parks** to take exercise or play games.
পার্ক

park verb
parks, parking, parked

When someone **parks** a car, they leave it somewhere.
গাড়ি পার্ক করা

They **parked** in the street outside the house.

parrot noun
parrots

A **parrot** is a bird with a curved beak and bright feathers.
টিয়াপাখি

Parrots' feet have two toes at the front and two at the back.

part noun
parts

Part of something is a piece of it.
অংশ

party noun
parties

A **party** is a time when people meet to have fun.
পার্টি

She's having a birthday **party**.

pass verb
passes, passing, passed

1. When you **pass** someone, you go by them.
   অতিক্রম করা

   We **passed** them on our way here.

2. If you **pass** something to someone, you give it to them.
   হস্তান্তরিত করা

   He **passed** a note to his friend.

3. If you **pass** a test, you do well.
   সাফল্যলাভ করা

passenger noun
passengers

A **passenger** is a person who is travelling in a vehicle, but who is not driving.
যাত্রী

pa st - pe as

past noun
The **past** is the period of time before now.
নাগালের বাহিরে
In the **past**, there weren't any computers.

past
1 Something that is **past** a place is on the other side of it.
পরে
It's just **past** the school there.
2 You use **past** when you are telling the time.
অতিবাহিত
It was ten **past** eleven.

pasta noun
Pasta is a mixture of flour, eggs, and water.
পাস্তা
Pasta comes in lots of shapes, even letters of the alphabet.

paste verb
pastes, pasting, pasted
1 If you **paste** something on to a surface, you stick it with glue.
সেঁটে দেওয়া
2 If you **paste** words or pictures on a computer, you copy them from one place and put them somewhere new.
পেস্ট
You can **paste** by holding down the Ctrl key and pressing V.

pastry noun
Pastry is a mixture of flour, butter, and water. People make it flat and thin so that they can use it to make pies.
কেক

path noun
paths
A **path** is a strip of ground that people walk along.
পথ
We followed the **path** along the cliff.

patient adjective
If you are **patient**, you don't get angry quickly.
ধৈর্যশীল

patient noun
patients
A **patient** is someone that a nurse or a doctor is looking after.
রোগী

pattern noun
patterns
A **pattern** is a group of repeated shapes.
নকশা
The carpet had a **pattern** of light and dark stripes.

paw noun
paws
The **paws** of an animal such as a cat, dog, or bear are its feet.
থাবা
The kitten was black with white **paws**.

pay verb
pays, paying, paid
If you **pay** for something, you give someone an amount of money for it.
মূল্য দেওয়া
Did you **pay** for those sweets?

peach noun
peaches
A **peach** is a round fruit with a soft red and orange skin.
পীচফল

peanut noun
peanuts
Peanuts are small nuts that you can eat.
চীনেবাদাম

pear noun
pears
A **pear** is a fruit which is narrow at the top and wide and round at the bottom.
নাসপাতি

peas noun
Peas are small, round, green vegetables.
মটর

98

pebble noun
pebbles
A **pebble** is a small, smooth stone.
নুড়ি

pedal noun
pedals
The **pedals** on a bicycle are the two parts that you push with your feet to make the bicycle move.
প্যাডেল

peel noun
The **peel** of a fruit is its skin.
খোসা

peg noun
pegs
A **peg** is a small piece of metal or wood on a wall that you hang things on.
গোঁজ/খোঁটা

pen noun
pens
A **pen** is a long thin tool that you use for writing with ink.
কলম

pencil noun
pencils
A **pencil** is a thin piece of wood with a black material through the middle that you use to write or draw with.
পেনসিল

penguin noun
penguins
A **penguin** is a black and white bird that lives in very cold places. **Penguins** can swim but they cannot fly.
পেঙ্গুইন

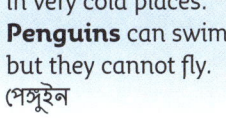

pentagon noun
pentagons
A **pentagon** is a shape with five straight sides.
পঞ্চভূজ

people noun
People are men, women, and children.
জনগণ

*Lots of **people** came to the party.*

pepper noun
peppers
1 **Pepper** is a powder with a hot taste that you put on food.
গোলমরিচ
2 A **pepper** is a green, red, or yellow vegetable with seeds inside it.
লঙ্কা

period noun
periods
A **period** is a length of time.
পর্ব

person noun
people
A **person** is a man, a woman, or a child.
ব্যক্তি

pest noun
pests
Pests are insects or small animals that damage crops or food.
পোকা

pet noun
pets
A **pet** is a tame animal that you keep in your home.
পোষ্য

99

pe**tal - pi**ll

petal noun
petals

The **petals** of a flower are the thin parts on the outside that are a bright colour.
পাপড়ি

phone noun
phones

A **phone** is a piece of equipment that you use to talk to someone in another place.
ফোন
Two minutes later the **phone** rang.

photograph noun
photographs

A **photograph** is a picture that you take with a camera.
ছবি
She took lots of **photographs** of her friends.

piano noun
pianos

A **piano** is a large instrument for playing music. You play it by pressing the black and white keys.
পিয়ানো

pick verb
picks, picking, picked

1 If you **pick** someone, you choose them.
বাছাই করা

2 When you **pick** flowers, fruit, or leaves, you take them from a plant or tree.
তোলা
I've **picked** some flowers from the garden.

picnic noun
picnics

When people have a **picnic**, they eat a meal outside, usually in a park or a forest, or at the beach.
পিকনিক
We're going on a **picnic** tomorrow.

picture noun
pictures

A **picture** is a drawing or painting.
চিত্র

pie noun
pies

A **pie** is a dish of fruit, meat, or vegetables that is covered with pastry and baked.
পিঠা/মাংসপুরিত পিঠা
We each had a slice of apple **pie**.

piece noun
pieces

A **piece** of something is a part of it.
টুকরো
You must only take one **piece** of cake.

pig noun
pigs

A **pig** is a farm animal with a fat body and short legs.
শুয়োর

pigeon noun
pigeons

A **pigeon** is a large grey bird.
পায়রা

pile noun
piles

A **pile** of things is several of them lying on top of each other.
স্তূপ
We searched through the **pile** of boxes.

pill noun
pills

Pills are small solid round pieces of medicine that you swallow.
বড়ি

pillow noun
pillows
A **pillow** is something soft that you rest your head on when you are in bed.
বালিশ

pilot noun
pilots
A **pilot** is a person who controls an aircraft.
বিমানচালক

pin noun
pins
A **pin** is a very small thin piece of metal with a point at one end.
পিন

pineapple noun
pineapples
A **pineapple** is a large sweet yellow fruit with a lot of juice. Its skin is brown, thick, and very rough.
আনারস

pipe noun
pipes
A **pipe** is a long tube that water or gas can flow through.
পাইপ
*They are going to take out the old water **pipes**.*

pirate noun
pirates
Pirates are people who attack ships and steal things from them.
জলদস্যু
*They have to find the **pirates** and the hidden gold.*

pizza noun
pizzas
A **pizza** is a flat, round piece of bread. **Pizzas** are covered with cheese and tomatoes.
পিৎজা
*Bake the **pizza** in a hot oven.*

place noun
places
1 A **place** is a building, area, town, or country.
স্থান
*This is the **place** where I was born.*

2 A **place** is also where something belongs.
অবস্থান
*He put the picture back in its **place** on the shelf.*

plain adjective
plainer, plainest
Something that is **plain** is ordinary and not special.
সাধারণ

plan noun
plans
A **plan** is a way of doing something that you work out before you do it.
পরিকল্পনা
*I've got a **plan** for getting out of here.*

plane noun
planes
A **plane** is a large vehicle with wings and engines that flies through the air.
বিমান

planet noun
planets
You find **planets** in space. They move around stars. The Earth is a **planet**.
গ্রহ

plant - pocket

plant noun
plants

A **plant** is a living thing that grows in the earth. **Plants** have a stem, leaves, and roots.
উদ্ভিদ

plaster noun
plasters

1 A **plaster** is a strip of material with a soft part in the middle. You can cover a cut on your body with a **plaster**.
প্লাস্টার

2 **Plaster** is a paste which people put on walls and ceilings so that they are smooth.
পলেস্তারা

*There were huge cracks in the **plaster**.*

plastic noun

Plastic is a material that is light but strong. It is made in factories.
প্লাস্টিক

*He put his sweets in a **plastic** bag.*

plate noun
plates

A **plate** is a flat dish that is used for holding food.
প্লেট

*She pushed her **plate** away.*

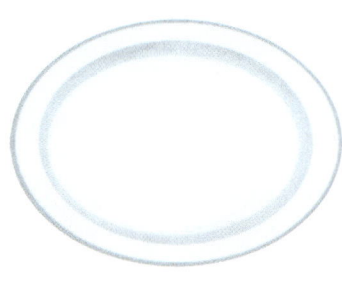

platform noun
platforms

A **platform** in a station is the place where you wait for a train.
প্ল্যাটফর্ম

play verb
plays, playing, played

1 When you **play**, you spend time using toys and taking part in games.
খেলা করা

*She was **playing** with her dolls.*

2 If you **play** an instrument, you make music with it.
বাজানো

playground noun
playgrounds

A **playground** is a special area where children can play.
খেলার মাঠ

please

You say **please** when you are asking someone to do something.
অনুগ্রহ করে

*Can you help us, **please**?*

plenty noun

If there is **plenty** of something, there is a lot of it.
প্রচুর

*Don't worry. There's still **plenty** of time.*

plough noun
ploughs

A **plough** is a large tool that is used on a farm. Farmers pull it across a field to make the earth loose, so that they can plant seeds.
লাঙ্গল

plus

You say **plus** to show that you are adding one number to another.
যুক্ত হওয়া

*Two **plus** two is four.*

pocket noun
pockets

A **pocket** is a small bag that is part of your clothes.
পকেট

*He put the key in his **pocket**.*

poem noun
poems

A **poem** is a piece of writing. When people write a **poem**, they choose the words in a very careful way, so that they sound beautiful.
কবিতা

point noun
points

1 The **point** of something is its thin, sharp end. Needles and knives have **points**.
ডগা

2 A **point** is a mark that you win in a game or a sport.
পয়েন্ট

point verb
points, pointing, pointed

If you **point** at something, you stick out your finger to show where it is.
উদ্দেশ্য করা

I pointed at the boy sitting near me.

poisonous adjective

Something that is **poisonous** will kill you or hurt you if you swallow or touch it.
বিষাক্ত

polar bear noun
polar bears

A **polar bear** is a large white bear which lives in the area around the North Pole.
শ্বেতভাল্লুক

police

The **police** are the people who make sure that people obey the law.
পুলিশ

polite adjective

Someone who is **polite** behaves well.
নম্র

pond noun
ponds

A **pond** is a small area of water.
পুকুর

We can feed the ducks on the pond.

pony noun
ponies

A **pony** is a small horse.
টাট্টু ঘোড়া

poor adjective
poorer, poorest

Someone who is **poor** doesn't have much money and doesn't own many things.
দরিদ্র

possible adjective

If something is **possible** it can happen.
সম্ভব

post verb
posts, posting, posted

If you **post** a letter, you put a stamp on it and send it to someone.
প্রেরণ করা

poster noun
posters

A **poster** is a large notice or picture that you stick on a wall.
বিজ্ঞাপনপত্র

potato noun
potatoes

Potatoes are hard round white vegetables with brown or red skins. They grow under the ground.
আলু

pour verb
pours, pouring, poured

If you **pour** something like water, you make it flow out of a container.
ঢালা

powder noun

Powder is a fine dry dust, like flour.
পাউডার

power noun

1 If someone has **power**, they have control over people.
ক্ষমতা
He has the **power** to keep you in after school.

2 The **power** of something is its strength.
শক্তি
The engine doesn't often work at full **power**.

practise verb
practises, practising, practised

If you **practise** something, you do it often in order to do it better.
অভ্যাস করা
I've been **practising** my song.

present noun
presents

1 The **present** is the period of time that is taking place now.
বর্তমান

2 A **present** is something that you give to someone for them to keep.
উপহার
She got a **present** for her birthday.

present adjective

If someone is **present** somewhere, they are there.
উপস্থিত
He wasn't **present** when they called out his name.

press verb
presses, pressing, pressed

If you **press** something, you push it hard.
টেপা
Press the blue button.

pretend verb
pretends, pretending, pretended

When you **pretend**, you act as if something is true, when you know it isn't.
ভান করা
She **pretended** to be the teacher.

pretty adjective
prettier, prettiest

If something is **pretty**, it is nice to look at.
সুন্দর
She was wearing a **pretty** necklace.

price noun
prices

The **price** of something is how much you have to pay to buy it.
মূল্য
Could you tell me the **price** of this car, please?

prick verb
pricks, pricking, pricked

If you **prick** something, you stick something sharp like a pin or a knife into it.
ফুটো করা
She **pricked** her finger on a pin.

prince noun
princes

A **prince** is a boy or a man in the family of a king or queen.
রাজকুমার

princess noun
princesses

A **princess** is a girl or a woman in the family of a king or queen.
রাজকুমারী

print - pudding

print verb
prints, printing, printed

1. If you **print** something, you use a machine to put words or pictures on paper.
ছাপা
2. If you **print** when you are writing, you do not join the letters together.
খোদাই করা

prison noun
prisons

A **prison** is a building where people who have broken the law are kept as a punishment.
কারাগার
*He was sent to **prison** for five years.*

prize noun
prizes

A **prize** is money or a special thing that you give to the person who wins a game, a race, or a competition.
পুরস্কার
*He won first **prize**.*

problem noun
problems

A **problem** is something or someone that makes thing difficult, or that makes you worry.
সমস্যা

program noun
programs

A **program** is a set of instructions that a computer uses to do a job.
কর্মসূচী

programme noun
programmes

A **programme** is a television or radio show.
অনুষ্ঠান
*She is watching her favourite television **programme**.*

project noun
projects

A **project** is a plan that takes a lot of time and effort.
প্রকল্প
*It was a large building **project**.*

promise verb
promises, promising, promised

If you **promise** to do something, you say that you will be sure to do it.
প্রতিশ্রুতি
*I **promise** that I'll help you all I can.*

pronoun noun
pronouns

A **pronoun** is a word that you use in place of a noun when you are talking about someone or something. "It" and "she" are **pronouns**.
সর্বনাম

proper adjective

The **proper** thing or way is the one that is right.
সঠিক
*Put things in their **proper** place.*

protect verb
protects, protecting, protected

If you **protect** something, you keep it safe.
রক্ষা করা
*Make sure you **protect** your skin from the sun.*

proud adjective
prouder, proudest

If you feel **proud**, you feel pleased about something good that you or other people close to you have done.
গর্বিত
*I was **proud** of our team today.*

pudding noun
puddings

A **pudding** is something sweet that you eat after your main meal.
পুডিং
*We had a delicious chocolate **pudding**.*

105

puddle - **py**ramid

puddle noun
puddles

A **puddle** is a small amount of water on the ground.
কাদামাখা ডোবা
Splashing in **puddles** is lots of fun.

pull verb
pulls, pulling, pulled

When you **pull** something, you hold it and move it towards you.
টানা
The dentist had to **pull** out all his teeth.

punishment noun
punishments

Punishment is something done to someone because they have done something wrong.
শাস্তি
His father sent him to bed early as a **punishment** for being rude.

pupil noun
pupils

The **pupils** at a school are the children who go there.
ছাত্র
Around 200 **pupils** go to this school.

puppet noun
puppets

A **puppet** is a small model of a person or animal that you can move.
তাঁরে চালীত পুতুলিকা

puppy noun
puppies

A **puppy** is a young dog.
কুকুরছানা

purple noun

Purple is a mixture of red and blue.
বেগুনী
Some grapes are **purple**.

purse noun
purses

A **purse** is a small bag that women use to carry money and other things.
টাকার ব্যাগ
She reached in her **purse** for her money.

push verb
pushes, pushing, pushed

When you **push** something, you press it in order to move it away from you.
পিছনে ঠেলা
I **pushed** back my chair and stood up.

put verb
puts, putting, put

When you **put** something somewhere, you move it there.
রাখা
He **put** the book on the desk.

puzzle verb
puzzles, puzzling, puzzled

If something **puzzles** you, you do not understand it and you feel confused.
বিভ্রান্ত করা
There was something about her that **puzzled** me.

pyjamas noun

Pyjamas are loose trousers and a jacket that you wear in bed.
পায়জামা

pyramid noun
pyramids

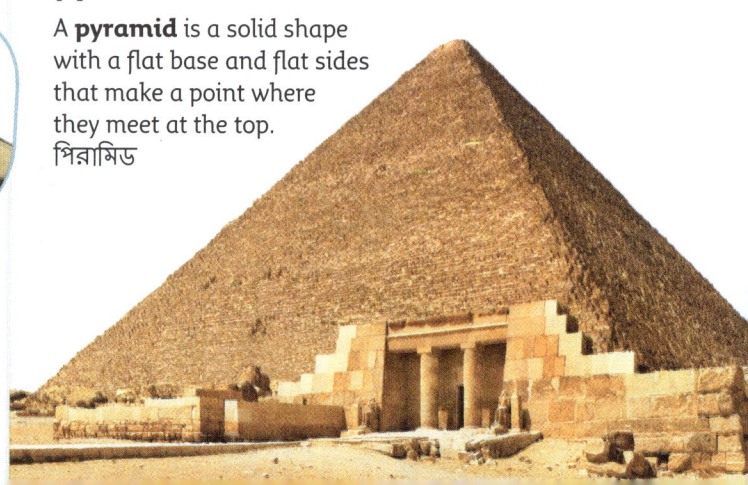

A **pyramid** is a solid shape with a flat base and flat sides that make a point where they meet at the top.
পিরামিড

106

Qq

quack verb
quacks, quacking, quacked

When a duck **quacks**, it makes a loud sound.
পাতিহাঁসের ডাক
There were ducks **quacking** on the lawn.

quarrel noun
quarrels

A **quarrel** is an angry argument between people.
ঝগড়া করা
I had an awful **quarrel** with my brothers.

quarter noun
quarters

A **quarter** is one of four equal parts of something.
এক-চতুর্থাংশ
My sister ate a **quarter** of the chocolate cake.

queen noun
queens

A **queen** is a woman who rules a country, or a woman who is married to a king.
রাণী
The crowd cheered when the **queen** went past.

question noun
questions

A **question** is something that you say or write to ask a person about something.
প্রশ্ন
They asked her a lot of **questions** about her holiday.

queue noun
queues

A **queue** is a line of people or cars waiting for something.
লাইন
He stood in the lunch **queue** for ten minutes.

quick adjective
quicker, quickest

Something that is **quick** moves or does things with great speed.
তাড়াতাড়ি
The cat was so **quick** that I couldn't catch it.

quickly

If you move or do something **quickly** you do it with great speed.
তাড়াতাড়ি করে
The girl ran **quickly** along the street.

quiet adjective
quieter, quietest

Someone who is **quiet** makes only a small amount of noise or no noise at all.
শান্ত
The baby was so **quiet** I didn't know he was there.

quite

Quite means a bit but not a lot.
বেশ
I **quite** like her but she's not my best friend.

quiz noun
quizzes

A **quiz** is a game in which someone asks you questions to find out what you know.
হেঁয়ালি/প্রহেলিকা
After dinner we had a TV **quiz** and our team won.

107

Rr

rabbit noun
rabbits
A **rabbit** is a small animal with long ears. **Rabbits** live in holes in the ground.
খরগোশ
The children were excited when they heard they were getting a pet **rabbit**.

race noun
races
A **race** is a competition to see who is fastest, for example in running or driving.
দৌড় প্রতিযোগিতা
Nobody can beat my sister in a **race**.

radiator noun
radiators
A **radiator** is a metal thing filled with hot water or steam. **Radiators** keep rooms warm.
রেডিয়েটর
I burned myself on the **radiator** in the bathroom.

radio noun
radios
A **radio** is a piece of equipment you use to hear programmes with talking, news and music.
বেতার
Turn on the **radio** for the news please.

railway noun
railways
A **railway** is a special road for trains, with stations along it. **Railways** have two metal lines that are always the same distance apart.
রেলওয়ে
The house was beside the **railway**.

rain noun
Rain is water that falls from the clouds in small drops.
বৃষ্টি
My mother told me not to go out in the **rain**.

rainbow noun
rainbows
A **rainbow** is a half circle of different colours in the sky. You can sometimes see a **rainbow** when it rains.
রামধনু
A **rainbow** appeared when the storm was over.

ran
➡ Look at **run**.
I **ran** to school because I was late.

rang
➡ Look at **ring**.
I got worried when the phone **rang**.

rare adjective
rarer, rarest
Something that is **rare** is not seen or heard very often.
বিরল
We are lucky to see this bird because it is very **rare**.

raspberry noun
raspberries
A **raspberry** is a small soft red fruit. **Raspberries** grow on bushes.
রাস্পবেরি ফল
Would you like some **raspberries** with your ice cream?

rat noun
rats
A **rat** is an animal that looks like a mouse. A **rat** has a long tail and sharp teeth.
ধেড়ে ইঁদুর
The old house was full of **rats**.

rather
You use **rather** to mean "a little bit".
বরং
I thought the party was **rather** boring.

raw adjective

Raw food has not been cooked.
কাঁচা

There is a bowl of **raw** carrots and cauliflower on the table.

reach verb
reaches, reaching, reached

1 When you **reach** a place, you arrive there.
পৌঁছানো

We will not **reach** home until midnight.

2 If you **reach** somewhere, you move your arm and hand to take or touch something.
নাগাল পাওয়া

I **reached** into my bag and brought out a pen.

read verb
reads, reading, read

When you **read**, you look at written words and understand them, and sometimes say them aloud.
পড়া

My father **reads** me a story every night before I go to sleep.

ready adjective

If you are **ready**, you are able to do something or go somewhere right now.
প্রস্তুত

It takes her a long time to get **ready** for school.

real adjective

1 Something that is **real** is true and is not imagined.
প্রকৃত

No, it wasn't a dream. It was **real**.

2 If something is **real**, it is not a copy.
খাঁটি

Is your necklace **real** gold?

really

1 You say **really** to show how much you mean something.
প্রকৃতপক্ষে

I'm **really** sorry I can't come to your party.

2 You say **really** to show that what you are saying is true.
সত্যসত্যই

Are we **really** going to the zoo?

reason noun
reasons

The **reason** for something is the fact which explains why it happens.
কারণ

You must have a good **reason** for being so late.

receive verb
receives, receiving, received

When you **receive** something, someone gives it to you, or you get it after it has been sent to you.
পাওয়া

Did you **receive** the birthday card I sent you?

recipe noun
recipes

A **recipe** is a list of food and a set of instructions telling you how to cook something.
রন্ধনপ্রণালী

Do you have a **recipe** for chocolate cake?

recite verb
recites, reciting, recited

When someone **recites** a poem or other piece of writing, they say it aloud after they have learned it.
আবৃত্তি করা

We each had to **recite** a poem in front of the class.

record noun
records

A **record** is the best result ever.
রেকর্ড

What's the world **record** for the 100 metres?

record verb
records, recording, recorded

If you **record** something like a TV programme, you make a copy of it so that you can watch it later.
রেকর্ড করা

Can you **record** the football for me please?

recorder noun
recorders

A **recorder** is a small instrument in the shape of a pipe. You play a **recorder** by blowing into it and putting your fingers over the holes in it.
রেকর্ডার

He has been learning the **recorder** for three years.

rectangle - rest

rectangle noun
rectangles

A **rectangle** is a shape with four straight sides.
আয়তক্ষেত্র

red noun

Red is the colour of blood or a strawberry.
লাল
Her dress is bright **red**.

reflection noun
reflections

A **reflection** is something you can see on a smooth, shiny surface. What you see is really in a different place.
প্রতিফলন
Reflections always show things the wrong way round.

refuse verb
refuses, refusing, refused

If you **refuse** to do something, you say that you will not do it.
প্রত্যাখ্যান করা
He **refuses** to have a bath.

remember verb
remembers, remembering, remembered

If you **remember** people or things from the past, you can bring them into your mind and think about them.
স্মরণ করা
I **remember** the first time I met him.

remind verb
reminds, reminding, reminded

If someone **reminds** you about something, they help you to remember it.
মনে করানো
Remind me to buy a bottle of milk, will you?

remove verb
removes, removing, removed

If you **remove** something from a place, you take it away.
অপসারণ করা
When the cake is cooked, **remove** it from the oven.

repair verb
repairs, repairing, repaired

If you **repair** something that is damaged or broken, you fix it so that it works again.
সারানো
The man managed to **repair** the broken tap.

repeat verb
repeats, repeating, repeated

If you **repeat** something, you say it, write it, or do it again.
আবার বলা
Please can you **repeat** the question?

reply verb
replies, replying, replied

If you **reply** to something, you say or write an answer.
উত্তর দেওয়া
Will you please **reply** when I ask you a question.

reptile noun
reptiles

A **reptile** is an animal that has cold blood, rough skin, and lays eggs. Snakes and lizards are **reptiles**.
সরীসৃপ

rescue verb
rescues, rescuing, rescued

If you **rescue** someone, you help them get away from a dangerous place.
উদ্ধার করা
The police **rescued** 20 people from the roof of the building.

rest verb
rests, resting, rested

If you **rest**, you sit or lie down and do not do anything active for a while.
আরাম করা
My grandmother always **rests** in the afternoon.

rest noun

The **rest** is the parts of something that are left.
বাকি
*Who ate the **rest** of the cake?*

restaurant noun
restaurants

A **restaurant** is a place where you can buy and eat a meal.
রেস্তোরাঁ
*We had lunch in an Italian **restaurant**.*

result noun
results

A **result** is something that happens because another thing has happened.
ফল
*I got measles and as a **result** was off school for two weeks.*

return verb
returns, returning, returned

1. When you **return** to a place, you go back to it after you have been away.
   ফিরে যাওয়া
   *He **returned** to Japan after his holiday in England.*

2. If you **return** something to someone, you give it back to them.
   ফিরিয়ে দেওয়া
   *I forgot to **return** my library books.*

reward noun
rewards

A **reward** is something that is given to a person because they have done something good.
পুরস্কার
*The school gives **rewards** to children who behave well.*

rhinoceros noun
rhinoceroses

A **rhinoceros** is a large wild animal with thick grey skin. A **rhinoceros** has one or two horns on its nose.
গণ্ডার

rhyme verb
rhymes, rhyming, rhymed

If two words **rhyme**, they have the same sound at the end of them.
ছড়া
*Sally **rhymes** with valley.*

rhythm noun
rhythms

Rhythm is something which is repeated again and again in the same way.
ছন্দ
*Listen to the **rhythm** of the music.*

rib noun
ribs

Your **ribs** are the 12 pairs of curved bones that go round your body.
পাঁজর
*He fell off his bike and broke a **rib**.*

ribbon noun
ribbons

A **ribbon** is a long narrow piece of cloth. You use **ribbons** to decorate things or tie them together.
ফিতে
*The girl's hair was tied with a blue and white **ribbon**.*

rice noun

Rice is white or brown grains from a plant. **Rice** grows in wet areas.
চাল
*The meal was chicken, **rice**, and vegetables.*

rich adjective
richer, richest

Someone who is **rich** has a lot of money and expensive things.
ধনী
*She is a **rich** woman who owns a very large house.*

riddle noun
riddles

A **riddle** is a question that seems to be nonsense, but that has a clever answer.
ধাঁধা
*He asked the **riddle**, "What key cannot open a door?" and I answered, "a monkey".*

111

ride - rode

ride verb
rides, riding, rode, ridden

When you **ride** a horse or a bike, you sit on it and control it as it moves along.
চড়া

The girl **rode** her horse along the beach.

right adjective

1 If something is **right**, it is correct and there have been no mistakes.
ঠিক

Only one child in the class knew the **right** answer to the teacher's question.

2 The **right** side is the side that is towards the east when you look north.
ডান

Most people write with their **right** hand.

ring verb
rings, ringing, rang, rung

When a bell **rings**, it makes a clear, loud sound.
বাজা

The school bell **rings** at nine o'clock.

ring noun
rings

A **ring** is a round piece of metal that you wear on a finger.
আংটি

He turned the **ring** on his finger.

ripe adjective
riper, ripest

When fruit or grain is **ripe**, it is ready to be eaten.
পাকা

Don't eat the apples until they are **ripe**.

rise verb
rises, rising, rose, risen

If something **rises**, it moves up.
ওপরে ওঠা

We watched the balloon **rise** into the sky.

river noun
rivers

A **river** is a long line of water that flows into the sea.
নদী

The Nile is one of the longest **rivers** in the world.

road noun
roads

A **road** is a long piece of hard ground for vehicles to travel on.
রাস্তা

You must look both ways before you cross the **road**.

roar verb
roars, roaring, roared

If a person, an animal or a thing **roars**, they make a very loud noise.
গর্জন করা

The engines **roared** and the aeroplane started to move.

robot noun
robots

A **robot** is a machine that can move and do things that it has been told to do.
রোবট

We have **robots** that we could send to the moon.

rock noun
rocks

1 **Rock** is the hard material that is in the ground and in mountains.
পাথর

We tried to dig, but the ground was solid **rock**.

2 A **rock** is a piece of this material.
শিলার টুকরো

She picked up a **rock** and threw it into the lake.

rock verb
rocks, rocking, rocked

If something **rocks**, it moves from side to side.
দোল খাওয়া

rocket noun
rockets

A **rocket** is a vehicle that people use to travel into space.
রকেট

This is the **rocket** that took them to the moon.

rode
⇨ Look at **ride**.

The man **rode** his bike down the hill.

roll *verb*
rolls, rolling, rolled
When something **rolls**, it moves along a surface, turning over and over.
গড়ানো
The ball bounced out of the garden and **rolled** across the road.

roof *noun*
roofs
The **roof** of a building is the bit on top that covers it.
ছাদ
Our house is the one with the red **roof**.

room *noun*
rooms
1 A **room** is a part of a building that has its own walls.
ঘর
A minute later he left the **room**.
2 If there is **room** somewhere, there is a enough empty space.
জায়গা
There isn't **room** for any more furniture in here.

root *noun*
roots
The **roots** of a plant are the parts of it that grow under the ground.
শিকড়
She dug a hole near the **roots** of an apple tree.

rope *noun*
ropes
A **rope** is a type of very thick string that is made by twisting together several strings or wires.
দড়ি
He tied the **rope** around his waist.

rose *noun*
roses
A **rose** is a large garden flower with a lovely smell. **Roses** grow on bushes.
গোলাপ ফুল
The teacher was given a bunch of red **roses**.

rough *adjective*
rougher, roughest
1 If something is **rough**, it is not smooth or even.
অসমান
His hands were **rough**.
2 If you are **rough**, you are not being careful or gentle.
অসভ্য/অভদ্র
Don't be so **rough** or you'll break it.

round *adjective*
rounder, roundest
Something **round** is in the shape of a ball or a circle.
গোল
There was a **round** table in the middle of the room.

row *noun*
rows
A **row** is a line of things or people.
সারি
Our house is opposite a **row** of shops.

rub *verb*
rubs, rubbing, rubbed
If you **rub** something, you move your hand or a cloth backwards and forwards over it.
ঘষা
I **rubbed** the window and looked outside.

rubber *noun*
rubbers
1 **Rubber** is a strong material that stretches. **Rubber** is used to make things like tyres and boots for wet weather.
রবার
2 A **rubber** is a small piece of rubber used to remove pencil mistakes.
রবার
Have you got a **rubber** in your pencil case?

113

rubbish - salt

rubbish noun
Rubbish is things like empty packs and used paper that you throw away.
আবর্জনা

rude adjective
ruder, rudest
If people are **rude**, they are not polite.
রূঢ়
It is **rude** to ask for something without saying "please".

ruin verb
ruins, ruining, ruined
If you **ruin** something, you destroy or spoil it.
নষ্ট করে দেওয়া
The rain **ruined** the party.

rule noun
rules
Rules are instructions that tell you what you must do or must not do.
নিয়ম
Can you explain the **rules** of cricket to me?

rule verb
rules, ruling, ruled
Someone who **rules** a country controls it.
রাজত্ব করা

ruler noun
rulers
1 A **ruler** is a long, flat piece of wood or plastic with straight edges. You use a **ruler** for measuring things or drawing straight lines.
রুলার
2 A **ruler** is also a person who rules a country.
শাসক
He was **ruler** of France at that time.

run verb
runs, running, ran, run
When you **run**, you move very quickly on your legs.
দৌড়ানো
It's very dangerous to **run** across the road.

rung
⇨ Look at **ring**.
They had **rung** the door bell when I was in the shower.

Ss

sad adjective
sadder, saddest
If you are **sad**, you don't feel happy.
দুঃখিত
I'm **sad** that he is leaving.

safe adjective
safer, safest
If you are **safe**, you are not in any danger.
সুরক্ষিত
Is it **safe**?

said
⇨ Look at **say**.
That is what she **said** to me.

sail noun
sails
Sails are large pieces of cloth on a boat that catch the wind and move the boat along.
পাল

salad noun
salads
A **salad** is a mixture of vegetables and sometimes other foods. You usually eat **salads** cold.
স্যালাড

salt noun
Salt is a white powder that you use to make food taste better.
নুন
Now add **salt** and pepper.

114

same *adjective*

If two things are the **same**, they are like one another.
এক রকম
*The two cats look the **same**.*

sand *noun*

Sand is a powder made of very small pieces of stone. Deserts and most beaches are made of **sand**.
বালু

sandal *noun*
sandals

Sandals are light shoes that you wear in warm weather.
চপ্পল
*He put on a pair of old **sandals**.*

sandwich *noun*
sandwiches

A **sandwich** is two slices of bread with another food such as cheese or meat between them.
স্যান্ডুইচ
*She ate a large **sandwich**.*

sang

⇨ Look at **sing**.
*She **sang** a happy song.*

sank

⇨ Look at **sink**.
*The boat **sank** in the storm.*

sari *noun*
saris

A **sari** is a long piece of material worn folded around the body by women.
শাড়ি
*She was wearing a new yellow **sari**.*

sat

⇨ Look at **sit**.
*She **sat** down next to the fire.*

satellite *noun*
satellites

A **satellite** is a machine that is sent into space to receive and send back information.
উপগ্রহ

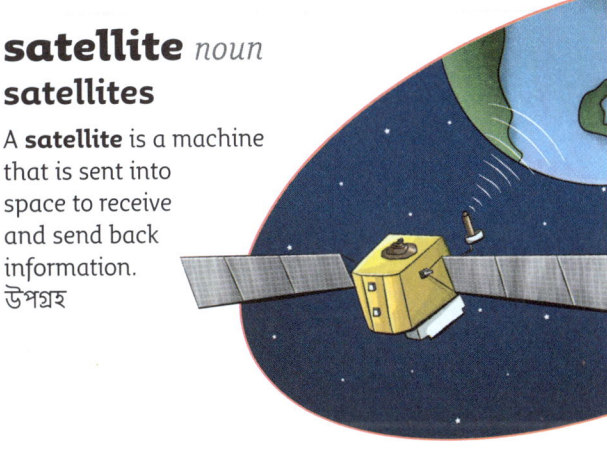

Saturday *noun*
Saturdays

Saturday is the day after Friday and before Sunday.
শনিবার
*He called her on **Saturday** morning.*

saucepan *noun*
saucepans

A **saucepan** is a deep metal container with a long handle and a lid. **Saucepans** are used for cooking.
সসপ্যান (পাত্র)
*Put the potatoes in a **saucepan** and boil them.*

saucer *noun*
saucers

A **saucer** is a small curved plate that you put under a cup.
চায়ের প্লেট

sausage - scream

A B C D E F G H I J K L M N O P Q R S T U V W X Y Z

sausage noun
sausages

A **sausage** is a mixture of very small pieces of meat and other foods, inside a long thin skin.
সসেজ

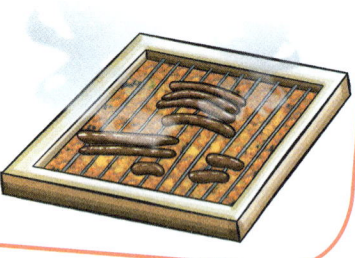

save verb
saves, saving, saved

1 If you **save** someone or something, you help them to escape from danger.
বাঁচানো
He **saved** the boy from drowning.

2 If you **save** something, you keep it because you will need it later.
বাঁচিয়ে রাখা
She was **saving** her money.

saw
⇨ Look at **see**.
We **saw** her walking down the street.

saw noun
saws

A **saw** is a metal tool for cutting wood.
করাত
He used a **saw** to cut the branches off the tree.

say verb
says, saying, said

When you **say** something, you talk.
বলা
She **said** that they were very pleased.

scale noun
scales

Scales are small, flat pieces of hard skin that cover the body of animals like fish and snakes.
মাছ বা সাঁপের আঁশ

scales noun

Scales are a machine used for weighing things.
তুলাযন্ত্র
He weighed flour on the **scales**.

scared adjective

If you are **scared** of something it frightens you.
ভীত
She is **scared** of spiders.

school noun
schools

A **school** is a place where people go to learn.
বিদ্যালয়
The **school** was built in the 1960s.

science noun
sciences

Science is the study of natural things.
বিজ্ঞান

scissors noun

Scissors are a small tool for cutting with two sharp parts that are joined together.
কাঁচি
Cut the card using **scissors**.

score verb
scores, scoring, scored

If you **score** in a game, you get a goal, run, or point.
স্কোর করা
He **scored** his second goal of the game.

scratch verb
scratches, scratching, scratched

1 If a sharp thing **scratches** someone or something, it makes small cuts on their skin or on its surface.
আঁচড়ে যাওয়া
The branches **scratched** my face.

2 If you **scratch** part of your body, you rub your nails against your skin.
চুলকানো
He **scratched** his head.

scream verb
screams, screaming, screamed

If you **scream**, you shout or cry in a loud, high voice.
চেঁচানো
She **screamed** when she saw the spider.

screen noun
screens
A **screen** is a flat surface on which a picture is shown.
পর্দা
There was dust on the television **screen**.

sea noun
seas
A **sea** is a large area of salt water.
সমুদ্র
They swam in the warm **sea**.

seal verb
seals, sealing, sealed
When you **seal** an envelope, you close it by folding part of it and sticking it down.
মোহর
He **sealed** the envelope and put on a stamp.

search verb
searches, searching, searched
If you **search** for something or someone, you look for them everywhere.
তল্লাসী
I am **searching** for my glasses.

seaside noun
The **seaside** is an area next to the sea.
সমুদ্রতীরে
I went to spend a few days at the **seaside**.

season noun
seasons
The **seasons** are the four parts of a year: spring, summer, autumn and winter.
ঋতু
Spring is my favourite **season**.

seat noun
seats
A **seat** is something that you can sit on.
আসন

second adjective
The **second** thing in a number of things is the one that you count as number two.
দ্বিতীয়
It was the **second** day of his holiday.

second noun
seconds
A **second** is an amount of time. There are sixty **seconds** in one minute.
সেকেন্ড
For a few **seconds** nobody spoke.

secret adjective
If something is **secret**, only a small number of people know about it, and they do not tell any other people.
গোপনীয়
He knew a **secret** place to hide in the garden.

see verb
sees, seeing, saw, seen
1 If you **see** something, you are looking at it or you notice it.
দেখা
The fog was so thick we couldn't **see** anything.

2 If you **see** someone, you meet them.
সাক্ষাৎ করা
I **saw** him yesterday.

seed noun
seeds
A **seed** is the small, hard part of a plant from which a new plant grows.
বীজ
Plant the **seeds** in the garden.

seem verb
seems, seeming, seemed
If something **seems** to be true, it appears to be true or you think it is true.
মনে হওয়া
The thunder **seemed** very close.

117

seen

⇨ Look at **see**.
She had **seen** the film before.

sell verb
sells, selling, sold

If you **sell** something, you let someone have it in return for money.
বিক্রি করা
The man **sold** his bike.

semicircle noun
semicircles

A **semicircle** is a half of a circle, or something with this shape.
অর্ধ গোলাকার
The children stood in a **semicircle**.

send verb
sends, sending, sent

When you **send** someone a message or a parcel, you make it go to them.
পাঠানো
I will **send** you a letter when I arrive.

sensible adjective

If you do something **sensible**, you have thought about it a lot first.
বিচারবুদ্ধি সম্পন্ন
The **sensible** thing is not to touch it.

sent

⇨ Look at **send**.
He **sent** a letter home.

September noun

September is the month after August and before October. It has 30 days.
সেপ্টেম্বর মাস

serve verb
serves, serving, served

Someone who **serves** customers in a shop or a restaurant helps them with what they want to buy.
পরিবেশন করা
She **served** me coffee and pie.

set noun
sets

A **set** of things is a number of things that belong together.
একরূপ দ্রব্যের সংগ্রহ
I'll need a **set** of clean clothes.

seven

Seven is the number 7.
সাত

several adjective

You use **several** for talking about a number of people or things that is not large but is greater than two.
অনেক
There were **several** boxes on the table.

sew verb
sews, sewing, sewed, sewn

When you **sew** pieces of cloth together, you join them using a needle and thread.
সেলাই করা
I must **sew** a button on to this shirt.

sex noun
sexes

The **sex** of a person or animal is if it is male or female.
লিঙ্গ
What **sex** is the baby?

118

shadow noun
shadows

A **shadow** is a dark shape on a surface that is made when something blocks the light.
ছায়া
The **shadows** of the trees crossed their path.

shake verb
shakes, shaking, shook, shaken

1. If you **shake** something, you hold it and move it quickly up and down.
ঝাঁকানো
Shake the bottle before you drink.

2. If someone or something **shakes**, they move quickly backwards and forwards or up and down.
কাঁপা
My body was **shaking** with cold.

shallow adjective
shallower, shallowest

If something is **shallow**, it is not deep.
অগভীর
The river is very **shallow** here.

shape noun
shapes

The **shape** of something is the way its outside edges or surfaces look.
আকার
Pasta comes in different **shapes** and sizes.

share verb
shares, sharing, shared

If you **share** something with another person, you both have it or use it.
ভাগ করে নেওয়া
We **shared** an ice cream.

shark noun
sharks

A **shark** is a very large fish. **Sharks** have very sharp teeth and some may attack people.
হাঙর মাছ

sharp adjective
sharper, sharpest

1. A **sharp** point or edge is very thin and can cut through things quickly.
ধারালো
Be careful, the scissors are **sharp**.

2. A **sharp** feeling is sudden and is very big or strong.
তীক্ষ্ণ
I felt a **sharp** pain in my right leg.

shave verb
shaves, shaving, shaved

If you **shave**, you remove hair from your face or body by cutting it off.
দাড়ি কামানো
Rahim took a bath and **shaved**.

shed noun
sheds

A **shed** is a small building where you store things.
কুঁড়েঘর
The house has a large **shed** in the garden.

she'd

1. **She'd** is short for **she had**.
তার (মহিলা) ছিল
She'd already seen them.

2. **She'd** is also short for **she would**.
তার (মহিলা) হবে
She'd be very happy.

sheep noun
sheep

A **sheep** is a farm animal with thick hair called wool. Farmers keep **sheep** for their wool or for their meat.
মেষ

sheet noun
sheets

1. A **sheet** is a large piece of cloth that you sleep on or cover yourself with in bed.
চাদর
Once a week, we change the **sheets**.

2. A **sheet** is a piece of paper, glass, plastic, or metal.
পাত
He folded the **sheets** of paper.

119

shelf - short

shelf noun
shelves

A **shelf** is a long flat piece of wood on a wall or in a cupboard that you can keep things on.
তাক
*Dad took a book from the **shelf**.*

shell noun
shells

1 The **shell** of an egg or nut is its hard part.
খোলা

2 The **shell** of an animal such as a snail is the hard part that covers its back and protects it.
খোলস

she'll

She'll is short for **she will**.
সে (মহিলা) হবে
She'll be back.

she's

She's is short for **she is**.
তিনি (মহিলা) হলেন
She's a doctor.

shine verb
shines, shining, shone

If something **shines**, it gives out bright light.
উজ্জ্বল হওয়া
*Today it's warm and the sun is **shining**.*

shiny adjective
shinier, shiniest

If something is **shiny**, it is bright.
উজ্জ্বল
*Her hair was **shiny** and clean.*

ship noun
ships

A **ship** is a large boat that carries people or things.
জাহাজ
*The **ship** was ready to leave.*

shirt noun
shirts

A **shirt** is something you wear on the top part of your body. It has a collar and buttons.
জামা

shiver verb
shivers, shivering, shivered

If you **shiver**, your body shakes because you are cold or scared.
ঠান্ডায় কাঁপা
*She **shivered** with cold.*

shoe noun
shoes

Shoes are a type of clothing that you wear on your feet.
জুতো
*I need a new pair of **shoes**.*

shone

⇨ Look at **shine**.
*The sun **shone** all day.*

shop noun
shops

A **shop** is a place that sells things.
দোকান
*He and his wife run a clothes **shop**.*

shore noun
shores

The **shore** of a sea or lake is the land along the edge of it.
তীর
*They walked slowly down to the **shore**.*

short adjective
shorter, shortest

1 If something is **short**, it does not last very long.
স্বল্পমেয়াদী
*Last year we all went to the seaside for a **short** holiday.*

2 A **short** thing is small in length, distance, or height.
ছোট
*She has **short**, straight hair.*

shorts noun

Shorts are trousers with short legs.
ছোট প্যান্ট
*He was wearing blue **shorts**.*

should verb

You use **should** when you are saying what is the right thing to do.
উচিত
*He **should** tell us what happened.*

shoulder noun
shoulders

Your **shoulders** are the two parts of your body between your neck and the tops of your arms.
কাঁধ
*Put your hands on the **shoulders** of the person in front of you.*

shout verb
shouts, shouting, shouted

If you **shout**, you say something in a very loud voice.
চিৎকার করা
*He **shouted** something to his brother.*

show verb
shows, showing, showed, shown

1 If you **show** someone something, you let them see it.
দেখানো
*She **showed** me her ring.*

2 If you **show** someone how to do something, you teach them how to do it.
প্রদর্শন করা
*She **showed** us how to make pasta.*

shower noun
showers

1 A **shower** is a thing that you stand under, that covers you with water so you can wash yourself.
স্নানার্থ কৃত্রিম বর্ষণযন্ত্র
*I was in the **shower** when the phone rang.*

2 A **shower** is a short period of rain.
একপশলা বৃষ্টি
*A few **showers** are expected tomorrow.*

shown

⇨ Look at **show**.
*I've **shown** them how to do it.*

shut verb
shuts, shutting, shut

If you **shut** something, you close it.
বন্ধ করা
*Please **shut** the gate.*

shy adjective
shyer, shyest

If you are **shy**, you are nervous about talking to people that you do not know well.
লাজুক
*She was a **shy**, quiet girl.*

sick adjective
sicker, sickest

If you are **sick**, you are not well.
অসুস্থ
*He's very **sick** and needs a doctor.*

side noun
sides

1 The **side** of something is a place to the left or right of it.
পাশ
*On the left **side** of the door there's a door bell.*

2 The **side** of something is also its edge.
দিক
*A square has four **sides**.*

3 The different **sides** in a game are the groups of people who are playing against each other.
দল
*Both **sides** want to win the match.*

121

sign - skies

A B C D E F G H I J K L M N O P Q R S T U V W X Y Z

sign noun
signs

1 A **sign** is a mark or a shape that has a special meaning.
চিহ্ন
In maths, **+** is a plus **sign** and **−** is a minus **sign**.

2 You can also make a **sign** to somebody by moving something.
সংকেত
They gave me a **sign** to show that everything was all right.

silent adjective

1 If you are **silent**, you are not talking.
চুপচাপ
She was **silent** because she did not know what to say.

2 If something is **silent**, it is quiet, with no sound at all.
নিস্তব্ধ
The room was **silent**.

silly adjective
sillier, silliest

If you are **silly**, you do not behave in a sensible way.
বোকা
Don't be **silly**!

silver noun

Silver is a valuable metal.
রুপো
He bought her a bracelet made from **silver**.

sing verb
sings, singing, sang, sung

When you **sing**, you make music with your voice.
গান করা
I love **singing**.

sink noun
sinks

A **sink** is a large fixed container in a kitchen or a bathroom that you can fill with water.
সিঙ্ক
The **sink** was filled with dirty dishes.

sister noun
sisters

Your **sister** is a girl or woman who has the same parents as you.
বোন
This is my **sister**.

sit verb
sits, sitting, sat

If you are **sitting** in a chair, your bottom is resting on the chair and the top part of your body is straight.
বসা
Mum was **sitting** in her chair in the kitchen.

six

Six is the number 6.
ছয়

size noun
sizes

The **size** of something is how big or small it is.
আকার
The **size** of the room is about five metres by seven metres.

skate noun
skates

Skates are boots with a thin metal bar on the bottom for moving quickly on ice.
দ্রুতবেগে বেড়াইবার পাদুকাবিশেষ

skeleton noun
skeletons

A **skeleton** is all the bones in a person's or animal's body.
কংকাল
A human **skeleton** has more than 200 bones.

skies

⇨ Look at **sky**.
The **skies** were grey.

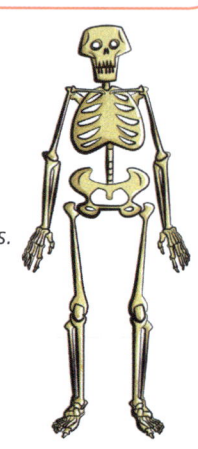

122

skill noun

If you have **skill** you are able to do something well.
দক্ষতা
He shows great **skill** on the football field.

skin noun
skins

1 Your **skin** covers your whole body.
চামড়া
Too much sun can damage your **skin**.

2 The **skin** of a fruit or vegetable covers the outside of it.
খোসা
She slipped on a banana **skin**.

skip verb
skips, skipping, skipped

1 If you **skip** along, you move along jumping from one foot to the other.
লাফিয়ে চলা
We **skipped** down the street.

2 If you **skip** something, you decide not to do it.
ছেড়ে দেওয়া
Don't **skip** breakfast.

skirt noun
skirts

A **skirt** is something that women and girls wear. It hangs down from the waist and covers part of the legs.
স্কার্ট

skull noun
skulls

A person's or animal's **skull** is the bones of their head.
মাথার খুলি
Your **skull** protects your brain.

sky noun
skies

The **sky** is the space around the Earth which you can see when you look up.
আকাশ
The sun was shining in the **sky**.

sleep verb
sleeps, sleeping, slept

If you **sleep**, you rest with your eyes closed and you do not move.
ঘুম
Be quiet! The baby is **sleeping**.

sleeve noun
sleeves

The **sleeves** of something you wear are the parts that cover your arms.
জামার হাতা
She wore a blue dress with long **sleeves**.

slept

⇨ Look at **sleep**.
She **slept** for three hours.

slice noun
slices

A **slice** of something is a thin piece that you cut from a larger piece.
ফালি
Would you like a **slice** of bread?

slide verb
slides, sliding, slid

When someone or something **slides**, they move quickly over a surface.
পিছলাইয়া যাওয়া
She **slid** across the ice on her stomach.

slip verb
slips, slipping, slipped

If you **slip**, you slide and fall.
পিছলে পড়া
He **slipped** on the wet grass.

slipper noun
slippers

Slippers are loose, soft shoes that you wear indoors.
চপ্পল
She put on a pair of **slippers**.

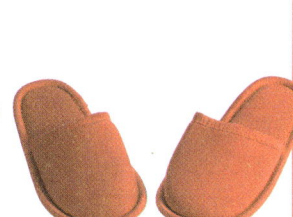

123

slippery - sneeze

slippery adjective
If something is **slippery**, it is smooth or wet, and is difficult to walk on or to hold.
পিছল
Be careful—the floor is **slippery**.

slope noun
slopes
A **slope** is the side of a mountain, hill, or valley.
ঢালু স্থান
A steep **slope** leads to the beach.

slow adjective
slower, slowest
If something is **slow**, it does not move quickly.
ধীরগতি
The bus was very **slow**.

slowly
If something moves **slowly**, it does not move quickly.
ধীরে ধীরে

slug noun
slugs
A **slug** is a small animal with a long soft body and no legs that moves very slowly.
খোলসহীন পোকা

small adjective
smaller, smallest
If something is **small**, it is not large in size or amount.
ছোট
She is **small** for her age.

smash verb
smashes, smashing, smashed
If you **smash** something, it breaks into many pieces.
ভেঙ্গে টুকরো টুকরো হওয়া
The plate **smashed** when it hit the floor.

smell noun
smells
The **smell** of something is what you notice about it when you breathe in through your nose.
গন্ধ
There was a horrible **smell** in the fridge.

smile verb
smiles, smiling, smiled
If you **smile**, the corners of your mouth turn up because you are happy or you think that something is funny.
মুচকে হাসা
He **smiled** at me.

smoke noun
Smoke is the black or white clouds of gas that you see in the air when something burns.
ধোঁয়া
Thick black **smoke** blew over the city.

smooth adjective
smoother, smoothest
Something **smooth** has no rough parts, lumps, or holes.
মসৃণ
The baby's skin was soft and **smooth**.

snail noun
snails
A **snail** is a small animal with a long, soft body, no legs, and a round shell on its back.
শামুক

snake noun
snakes
A **snake** is a long, thin animal with no legs, that slides along the ground.
সাপ

sneeze verb
sneezes, sneezing, sneezed
When you **sneeze**, you suddenly take in air and then blow it down your nose in a noisy way.
হাঁচি
Cover your nose and mouth when you **sneeze**.

snow noun

Snow is pieces of soft white frozen water that fall from the sky.
তুষার
Six inches of **snow** fell last night.

soap noun

Soap is something that you use with water for washing yourself.
সাবান
She bought a bar of **soap**.

sock noun
socks

Socks are pieces of cloth that you wear over your foot and ankle, inside your shoes.
মোজা
I have a pair of red **socks**.

sofa noun
sofas

A **sofa** is a long, comfortable seat with a back, that two or three people can sit on.
সোফা (আসবাব পত্র)

soft adjective
softer, softest

1 Something that is **soft** is nice to touch, and not rough or hard.
নরম
She wiped the baby's face with a **soft** cloth.

2 A **soft** sound or light is very gentle.
কোমল
There was a **soft** tapping on my door.

soil noun

Soil is the top layer on the surface of the earth in which plants grow.
মাটি
The **soil** here is good for growing vegetables.

sold
⇨ Look at **sell**.
They **sold** their house today.

soldier noun
soldiers

A **soldier** is someone who is in an army.
সৈনিক

solid adjective

1 Something that is **solid** stays the same shape if it is in a container or not.
কঠিন

2 Something that is **solid** is not hollow.
নিরেট
They had to cut through 5 feet of **solid** rock.

some

You use **some** to talk about an amount of something.
কিছুটা
Can I have **some** orange juice please?

somebody

You use **somebody** to talk about a person without saying who you mean.
কেউ

someone

You use **someone** to talk about a person without saying who you mean.
কোন একজন
I need **someone** to help me.

something

You use **something** to talk about a thing without saying what it is.
কিছু জিনিস
He knew that there was **something** wrong.

sometimes

You use **sometimes** to talk about things that do not take place all the time.
কখনো কখনো
Sometimes he's a little rude.

somewhere - speak

somewhere
You use **somewhere** to talk about a place without saying where you mean.
কোনখানে
*I've seen him before **somewhere**.*

son noun
sons
Someone's **son** is their male child.
পুত্র
*His **son** is seven years old.*

song noun
songs
A **song** is words and music sung together.
গান
*She sang a **song**.*

soon adjective
sooner, soonest
If you are going to do something **soon** you will do it a very short time from now.
শীঘ্র
*I'll call you **soon**.*

sore adjective
sorer, sorest
If part of your body is **sore**, it is painful.
ক্ষত
*I had a **sore** throat.*

sorry adjective
sorrier, sorriest
1. If you are **sorry** about something, you feel sad about it.
দুঃখিত
*I'm **sorry** he's gone.*
2. If you feel **sorry** for someone, you feel sad for them.
দুঃখিত
*I felt **sorry** for him because nobody listened to him.*

sort noun
sorts
The different **sorts** of something are the different types of it.
ধরণ
*What **sort** of school do you go to?*

sound noun
sounds
A **sound** is something that you hear.
শব্দ
*He heard the **sound** of a car engine outside.*

soup noun
Soup is liquid food made by boiling meat, fish, or vegetables in water.
সুপ, ঝোল

sour adjective
Something that is **sour** has a sharp, nasty taste.
টক
*Lemons have a **sour** taste.*

south noun
The **south** is the direction to your right when you are looking towards the place where the sun rises.
দক্ষিণ দিক

space noun
spaces
1. You use **space** to talk about an area that is empty.
থালি জায়গা
*They cut down trees to make **space** for houses.*
2. **Space** is the area past the Earth, where the stars and planets are.
মহাকাশ
*The six astronauts will spend ten days in **space**.*

spade noun
spades
A **spade** is a tool that is used for digging.
কোদাল

speak verb
speaks, speaking, spoken
When you **speak**, you say words.
বলা
*He **spoke** in a whisper.*

126

special adjective

Someone or something that is **special** is better or more important than other people or things.
বিশেষ

*Mum made a **special** cake for my birthday.*

speed noun
speeds

The **speed** of something is how fast it moves or is done.
গতি

*He drove off at high **speed**.*

spell verb
spells, spelling, spelled or spelt

When you **spell** a word, you write or say each letter in the correct order.
উচ্চারণ করা

*He **spelled** his name.*

spend verb
spends, spending, spent

1 When you **spend** money, you buy things with it.
ব্যয় করা
*I have **spent** all my money.*

2 To **spend** time or energy is to use it doing something.
অতিবাহিত করা
*She **spends** hours working on her garden.*

spider noun
spiders

A **spider** is a small animal with eight legs.
মাকড়সা

spill verb
spills, spilling, spilled or spilt

If you **spill** a liquid, you make it flow over the edge of a container by accident.
ছড়িয়ে পড়া

*He always **spilled** the drinks.*

spin verb
spins, spinning, spun

If something **spins**, it turns around quickly.
ঘোরা

*He made the coin **spin** on his desk.*

spine noun
spines

Your **spine** is the row of bones down your back.
শিরদাঁড়া

splash verb
splashes, splashing, splashed

If you **splash** in water, you hit the water in a noisy way.
জল ছিটান

*The children **splashed** around in the water.*

spoil verb
spoils, spoiling, spoiled or spoilt

1 If you **spoil** something, you damage it or stop it from working as it should.
নষ্ট করা
*Don't **spoil** the surprise.*

2 If you **spoil** children, you give them everything they want or ask for.
নষ্ট করে দেওয়া
*She acted like a **spoilt** child.*

127

spoke noun
spokes

The **spokes** of a wheel are the bars which join the outside ring to the centre.
চাকার স্পোক

spoke
➪ Look at **speak**.
She **spoke** in a loud voice.

spoken
➪ Look at **speak**.
He has **spoken** to us.

spoon noun
spoons

A **spoon** is a long tool with a round end that is used for eating, serving or mixing food.
চামচ
He stirred his coffee with a **spoon**.

sport noun
sports

Sports are games which need energy and skill.
ক্রীড়া
She is very good at **sport**.

spot noun
spots

Spots are small, round areas on a surface.
গোল দাগ
The leaves are yellow with orange **spots**.

spot verb
spots, spotting, spotted

If you **spot** something or someone, you notice them.
লক্ষ্য করা
I didn't **spot** the mistake in his work.

spout noun
spouts

A **spout** is a tube for pouring liquid.
মুখনল
My kettle has a long **spout**.

spray noun
sprays

Spray is a lot of small drops of water that are thrown into the air.
ছড়ানো
The **spray** from the waves covered them.

spread verb
spreads, spreading, spread

1. If you **spread** something somewhere, you open it out.
ছড়িয়ে দেওয়া
She **spread** a towel on the sand and lay on it.

2. If you **spread** something on a surface, you put it all over the surface.
ছড়িয়ে দেওয়া
She was **spreading** butter on the bread.

3. If something **spreads**, it reaches a larger area.
ছড়িয়ে যাওয়া
The news **spread** quickly.

spring noun
springs

1. **Spring** is the season between winter and summer when the weather becomes warmer and plants start to grow again.
বসন্তকাল
They are getting married next **spring**.

2. A **spring** is a long piece of metal that goes round and round. It goes back to the same shape after you pull it.
স্প্রিং
The **springs** in the bed were old.

spun
➪ Look at **spin**.
He **spun** the wheel.

square noun
squares

A **square** is a shape with four straight sides that are all the same length.
বর্গক্ষেত্র
Cut the cake in **squares**.

squirrel noun
squirrels

A **squirrel** is a small animal with a long thick tail. **Squirrels** live in trees.
কাঠবিড়ালী

stable - steal

stable noun
stables

A **stable** is a building where people keep horses.
আস্তাবল

stairs noun

Stairs are steps you walk down or up in a building.
সিঁড়ি
He walked up the **stairs**.

stamp noun
stamps

A **stamp** is a small piece of paper that you stick on an envelope before you post it.
ডাকটিকিট
She put a **stamp** on the corner of the envelope.

stamp verb
stamps, stamping, stamped

If you **stamp** your foot, you put your foot down very hard on the ground.
মাটিতে ঠোকা
I **stamped** my feet to keep warm.

stand verb
stands, standing, stood

When you are **standing**, you are on your feet.
দাঁড়ান
She was **standing** beside my bed.

star noun
stars

1 A **star** is a large ball of burning gas in space. **Stars** look like small points of light in the sky.
নক্ষত্র
Stars lit the sky.

2 A **star** is a shape that has four, five, or more points sticking out of it in a pattern.
তারকা চিহ্ন
How many **stars** are there on the flag?

3 A **star** is somebody who is famous for doing something, for example acting or singing.
তারকা
He's one of the **stars** of a TV show.

start verb
starts, starting, started

1 When something **starts**, it begins.
শুরু হওয়া
When does the film **start**?

2 If you **start** to do something, you begin to do it.
শুরু করা
She **started** to read her book.

station noun
stations

A **station** is a place where trains or buses stop so that people can get on or off.
রেল স্টেশন
We went to the train **station**.

stay verb
stays, staying, stayed

1 If you **stay** in a place, you do not move away from it.
থাকা
She **stayed** in bed until noon.

2 If you **stay** somewhere, you live there for a short time.
কোথাও থাকা
He **stayed** with them for two weeks.

steady adjective
steadier, steadiest

Something that is **steady** is firm and not shaking.
দৃঢ়
He held out a **steady** hand.

steal verb
steals, stealing, stole, stolen

If you **steal** something from someone, you take it without asking or telling them and don't give it back.
চুরি করা
They said he **stole** a bicycle.

129

steam - stolen

steam noun
Steam is the hot gas that water becomes when it boils.
বাষ্প
The **steam** rose into the air.

steel noun
Steel is a very strong metal that is made from iron.
ইস্পাত
The door is made of **steel**.

steep adjective
steeper, steepest
A **steep** slope rises quickly and is difficult to go up.
খাড়া
Some of the hills are very **steep**.

stem noun
stems
The **stem** of a plant is the long, thin part that the flowers and leaves grow on.
কান্ড/ডাল
He cut the **stem** and gave her the flower.

step noun
steps
1 If you take a **step**, you lift your foot and put it down in a different place.
ধাপ
I took a **step** towards him.
2 A **step** is a flat surface that you put your feet on to walk up or down to somewhere.
পদক্ষেপ ফেলা
We went down the **steps** into the garden.

stick noun
sticks
A **stick** is a long, thin piece of wood.
লাঠি
She put some dry **sticks** on the fire.

stick verb
sticks, sticking, stuck
If you **stick** one thing to another, you join them together using glue.
আটকানো
Now **stick** your picture on a piece of paper.

stiff adjective
stiffer, stiffest
Something that is **stiff** is firm and is not easy to bend.
শক্ত
The sheet of cardboard was **stiff**.

still adjective
stiller, stillest
If you are **still**, you are not moving.
নিশ্চল
Please stand **still**.

sting verb
stings, stinging, stung
If a plant, an animal, or an insect **stings** you, a part of it is pushed into your skin so that you feel a sharp pain.
হুল ফোটানো
She was **stung** by a bee.

stir verb
stirs, stirring, stirred
When you **stir** a liquid, you move it around using a spoon or a stick.
নাড়ান

stole
⇨ Look at **steal**.
They **stole** our car last night.

stolen
⇨ Look at **steal**.
All of her money was **stolen**.

stomach noun
stomachs

Your **stomach** is the place inside your body where food goes when you eat it.
পাকস্থলী
His **stomach** felt full after the meal.

stone noun
stones

1 **Stone** is a hard solid material that is found in the ground. It is often used for building.
পাথর
The floor was solid **stone**.

2 A **stone** is a small piece of rock that is found on the ground.
কাঁকর
He took a **stone** out of his shoe.

stood

⇨ Look at **stand**.
He **stood** in the street.

stop verb
stops, stopping, stopped

1 If you **stop** doing something, you do not do it any more.
থামানো
Stop throwing those stones!

2 If something **stops**, it does not do what it did any more.
বন্ধ হওয়া
The rain has **stopped**.

store verb
stores, storing, stored

If you **store** something, you keep it somewhere safe.
মজুদ করা

storm noun
storms

A **storm** is very bad weather, with heavy rain and strong winds.
ঝড়
There will be **storms** along the East Coast.

stomach - stream

story noun
stories

When someone tells you a **story** they describe people and things that are not real, in a way that makes you enjoy hearing about them.
গল্প
I'm going to tell you a **story** about four little rabbits.

straight adjective
straighter, straightest

If something is **straight**, it goes one way and does not bend.
সোজা
The boat moved in a **straight** line.

strange adjective
stranger, strangest

Something that is **strange** is unusual.
অদ্ভুত
I had a **strange** dream last night.

straw noun
straws

1 **Straw** is the dry, yellow stems of crops.
খড়
The floor of the barn was covered with **straw**.

2 A **straw** is a thin tube that you use to suck a drink into your mouth.
সরু নল
I drank my milk through a **straw**.

strawberry noun
strawberries

A **strawberry** is a small soft red fruit that has a lot of very small seeds on its skin.
স্ট্রবেরি ফল

stream noun
streams

A **stream** is a small narrow river.
জল স্রোত
There was a **stream** at the end of the garden.

131

street - submarine

street noun
streets

A **street** is a road in a city or a town.
রাস্তা
The **streets** were full of people.

strength noun

Your **strength** is how strong you are.
শক্তি
Swimming builds up the **strength** of your muscles.

stretch verb
stretches, stretching, stretched

1 Something that **stretches** over an area covers all of it.
প্রসারিত হওয়া
The line of cars **stretched** for miles.

2 When you **stretch**, you hold out part of your body as far as you can.
ছড়িয়ে দেওয়া
He yawned and **stretched**.

strict adjective
stricter, strictest

A **strict** person expects people to obey rules.
কঠোর
My parents are very **strict**.

string noun
strings

1 **String** is thin rope that is made of twisted threads.
সরু দড়ি
He held out a small bag tied with **string**.

2 The **strings** on an instrument are the thin pieces of wire that are stretched across it and that make sounds when the instrument is played.
তার
He changed a guitar **string**.

strip noun
strips

A **strip** of something is a long, narrow piece of it.
পাতলা ফালি
Cut a **strip** off a piece of paper, then twist it and stick the two ends together. Then cut it along the middle and see what happens.

stripe noun
stripes

A **stripe** is a long line that is a different colour from the areas next to it.
সরু সরু রেখা
She wore a blue skirt with white **stripes**.

strong adjective
stronger, strongest

1 Someone who is **strong** is healthy with good muscles.
সবল
I'm not **strong** enough to carry him.

2 **Strong** things are not easy to break.
শক্ত
This **strong** plastic will not crack.

stuck adjective

1 If something is **stuck** in a place, it cannot move.
দাঁড়িয়ে যাওয়া
His car got **stuck** in the snow.

2 If you get **stuck**, you can't go on doing something because it is too difficult.
আটকে যাওয়া
The teacher will help if you get **stuck**.

stung
⇨ Look at **sting**.
He was **stung** by a wasp.

submarine noun
submarines

A **submarine** is a ship that can travel under the sea.
ডুবোজাহাজ

132

subtraction noun

Subtraction is when you take one number away from another.
বিয়োগ

suck verb
sucks, sucking, sucked

If you **suck** something, you hold it in your mouth for a long time.
চোষা
They **sucked** their sweets.

sudden adjective

Something **sudden** is quick and is not expected.
হঠাৎ
The car came to a **sudden** stop.

suddenly

Suddenly is quickly, without being expected.
হঠাৎ করে
Suddenly there was a loud bang.

sugar noun

Sugar is a sweet thing that is used for making food and drinks taste sweet.
চিনি
Do you take **sugar** in your coffee?

suit noun
suits

A **suit** is a jacket and trousers or a skirt that are made from the same cloth.
পরিধানের স্যুট
He was wearing a dark **suit**.

sum noun
sums

1. A **sum** of money is an amount of money.
   টাকার পরিমাণ
   Large **sums** of money were lost.
2. In maths, a **sum** is a problem you work out using numbers.
   অঙ্ক
   I have to finish these **sums**.

summer noun
summers

Summer is the season after spring and before autumn. In the **summer** the weather is usually warm or hot.
গ্রীষ্মকাল

sun noun
suns

The **sun** is the large ball of burning gas in the sky that gives us light.
সূর্য
The **sun** was now high in the sky.

Sunday noun
Sundays

Sunday is the day after Saturday and before Monday.
রবিবার
We went for a drive on **Sunday**.

sunflower noun
sunflowers

A **sunflower** is a very tall plant with large yellow flowers.
সূর্যমুখী

sung

⇨ Look at **sing**.
She has **sung** the song many times before.

sunk

⇨ Look at **sink**.
The rock has **sunk** to the bottom of the river.

sunny adjective
sunnier, sunniest

When it is **sunny**, the sun is shining.
রৌদ্রোজ্জ্বল
The weather was warm and **sunny**.

133

sunshine noun

Sunshine is the light that comes from the sun.
সূর্যকিরণ
*She was sitting outside in bright **sunshine**.*

supermarket noun
supermarkets

A **supermarket** is a large shop that sells all kinds of food and other things for the home.
বড়দোকান
*Lots of people buy food in a **supermarket**.*

sure adjective

If you are **sure** that something is true, you know that it is true.
নিশ্চিত
*I am **sure** my answer is correct.*

surface noun
surfaces

The **surface** of something is the flat top part of it or the outside of it.
উপরিভাগ
*There were pen marks on the table's **surface**.*

surname noun
surnames

Your **surname** is your last name which you share with other people in your family.
পদবী

surprise noun
surprises

A **surprise** is something that you do not expect.
বিস্ময়
*I have a **surprise** for you!*

swallow verb
swallows, swallowing, swallowed

If you **swallow** something, you make it go from your mouth down into your stomach.
গিলে ফেলা
*She took a bite of the apple and **swallowed** it.*

swam

⇨ Look at **swim**.
*She **swam** across the river.*

swan noun
swans

A **swan** is a large bird with a long neck, that lives on rivers and lakes.
রাজহংস

sweep verb
sweeps, sweeping, swept

If you **sweep** an area, you push dirt off it using a brush with a long handle.
ঝাড়ু দেওয়া
*The man in the shop was **sweeping** the floor.*

sweet adjective
sweeter, sweetest

Sweet food and drink has a lot of sugar in it.
মিষ্টি
*Mum gave me a cup of **sweet** tea.*

sweet noun
sweets

Sweets are foods that have a lot of sugar.
মিষ্টি খাবার
*Don't eat too many **sweets**.*

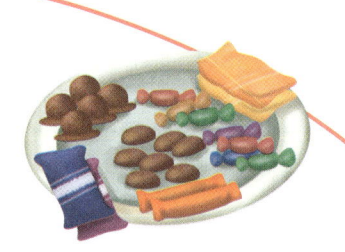

swept
⇨ Look at **sweep**.
The rubbish was **swept** away.

swim *verb*
swims, swimming, swam, swum
When you **swim**, you move through water by moving your arms and legs.
সাঁতার কাটা
She learned to **swim** when she was three.

swing *verb*
swings, swinging, swung
If something **swings**, it keeps moving backwards and forwards or from side to side through the air.
দোলানো
She walked beside him with her arms **swinging**.

switch *noun*
switches
A **switch** is a small button for turning something on or off.
বিদ্যুতের সুইচ
She pressed the **switch** to turn on the light.

sword *noun*
swords
A **sword** is like a long knife, with a handle and a long sharp blade.
তরবারি

swum
⇨ Look at **swim**.
He had never **swum** so far.

swung
⇨ Look at **swing**.
She **swung** her bag backwards and forwards.

Tt

table *noun*
tables
A **table** is a piece of furniture that has legs and a flat top.
টেবিল

tadpole *noun*
tadpoles
A **tadpole** is a small black animal with a round head and a long tail that lives in water. **Tadpoles** grow into frogs or toads.
ব্যাঙাচি

tail *noun*
tails
An animal's **tail** is the long, thin part at the end of its body.
লেজ

take *verb*
takes, taking, took, taken
1. If you **take** something, you move it or carry it.
   নেওয়া
   She **took** the plates into the kitchen.
2. If you **take** something that does not belong to you, you steal it.
   হস্তগত করা
   Someone **took** all our money.
3. If you **take** a vehicle, you ride in it from one place to another.
   যানবাহনে চড়া
   We **took** the bus to school.

talk *verb*
talks, talking, talked
When you **talk**, you say things to someone.
কথা বলা
She **talked** to him on the phone.

tall adjective
taller, tallest

If a person or thing is **tall**, they are higher than usual from top to bottom.
লম্বা

*It was a very **tall** building.*

tame adjective
tamer, tamest

If an animal or bird is **tame**, it is not afraid of people and will not try to hurt them.
গৃহপালিত

tap verb
taps, tapping, tapped

If you **tap** something, you hit it but you do not use a lot of strength.
আস্তে আস্তে স্পর্শ করা

*He **tapped** on the door and went in.*

tape noun

Tape is a long, thin strip of plastic that has glue on one side. You use **tape** to stick things together.
এক দিকে আঠা লাগানো প্লাস্টিকের ফিতা

*He wrapped the parcel with paper and **tape**.*

taste verb
tastes, tasting, tasted

If you **taste** something, you eat or drink a small amount of it to see what it is like.
স্বাদ নেওয়া

*She **tasted** the soup and then added some salt.*

taught

➩ Look at **teach**.
*My mum **taught** me to read.*

tea noun

1 **Tea** is a drink. You make it by pouring hot water on to the dry leaves of a plant called the **tea** bush.
চা

2 **Tea** is also a meal that you eat in the afternoon or the early evening.
চা-পান

teach verb
teaches, teaching, taught

If you **teach** someone something, you help them to understand it or you show them how to do it.
পড়ানো

*He **teaches** people how to play the piano.*

teacher noun
teachers

A **teacher** is a person whose job is to teach other people. **Teachers** usually work in schools.
শিক্ষক

team noun
teams

A **team** is a group of people who work together, or who play a sport together against another group.
দল

*He is in the school football **team**.*

tear noun
tears

Tears are the liquid that comes out of your eyes when you cry.
অশ্রু

*Her face was wet with **tears**.*

tear verb
tears, tearing, tore, torn

If you **tear** something, you pull it into pieces or make a hole in it.
ছিঁড়ে ফেলা

*Try not to **tear** the paper.*

teeth
➡ Look at **tooth**.
Clean your **teeth** before you go to bed.

telephone noun
telephones

A **telephone** is a machine that you use to talk to someone who is in another place.
দূরকথন যন্ত্র/দূরভাষ

television noun
televisions

A **television** is a machine that shows moving pictures with sound on a screen.
দূরদর্শন

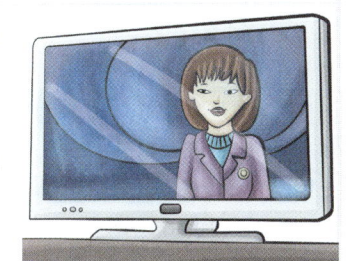

tell verb
tells, telling, told

1. If you **tell** someone something, you let them know about it.
বলা
Tell me about your holiday.

2. If you **tell** someone to do something, you say that they must do it.
বলা
She **told** me to go away.

3. If you can **tell** something, you know it.
বলতে পারা
I can **tell** that he is angry.

ten noun
Ten is the number 10.
দশ

tent noun
tents

A **tent** is made of strong material that is held up with long pieces of metal and ropes. You sleep in a **tent** when you stay in a camp.
তাঁবু

term noun
terms

A **term** is one of the parts of a school year. There are usually three **terms** in a year.
পর্ব

terrible adjective
If something is **terrible**, it is very bad.
সাংঘাতিক
That was a **terrible** film.

test verb
tests, testing, tested

If you **test** something, you try it to see what it is like, or how it works.
পরীক্ষা করা
Test the water to see if it is warm.

test noun
tests

A **test** is something you do to show how much you know or what you can do.
পরীক্ষা
The teacher gave us a maths **test**.

thank verb
thanks, thanking, thanked

When you **thank** someone, you tell them that you are pleased about something they have given you or have done for you. You usually do this by saying "Thank you".
ধন্যবাদ দেওয়া
I **thanked** him for my present.

theatre noun
theatres

A **theatre** is a building where you go to see people acting stories, singing, or dancing.
রঙ্গমঞ্চ

their

You use **their** to say that something belongs to a group of people, animals, or things.
তাদের
They took off **their** coats.

theirs

You use **theirs** to say that something belongs to a group of people, animals, or things.
কেবলমাত্র তাদের
The house next to **theirs** was empty.

then

1 **Then** means at that time.
   তখন
   He wasn't as rich **then** as he is now.

2 You also use **then** to say that one thing happens after another.
   তারপর
   She said good night, **then** went to bed.

there

1 You use **there** to say that something is in a place or is happening, or to make someone notice it.
   কোন জায়গায়
   There are flowers on the table.

2 **There** also means to a place, or at a place.
   সেখানে
   I have never been **there** before.

there's

There's is short for **there is**.
সেখানে
There's nothing in the box.

they

You use **they** when you are talking about more than one person, animal, or thing.
তাহারা
They are all in the same class.

they'd

1 **They'd** is short for **they had**.
   তাদের ছিল

2 **They'd** is also short for **they would**.
   তারা করবে
   The boys said **they'd** come back later.

they'll

They'll is short for **they will**.
তারা করবে
They'll be here on Monday.

they're

They're is short for **they are**.
তারা হবে
They're going to the circus.

they've

They've is short for **they have**.
তাদের আছে
They've gone away.

thick adjective
thicker, thickest

1 If something is **thick**, it is deep or wide between one side and the other.
   গুরু/মোটা
   He cut a **thick** slice of bread.

2 If a liquid is **thick**, it flows slowly.
   ঘন
   This soup is very **thick**.

thigh noun
thighs

Your **thighs** are the parts of your legs that are above your knees.
উরু
His **thighs** ached from climbing the hill.

thin adjective
thinner, thinnest

1 If something is **thin**, it is narrow between one side and the other.
   পাতলা
   The book is printed on very **thin** paper.

2 If a person or animal is **thin**, they are not fat and they do not weigh much.
   রোগা
   He was a tall, **thin** man.

thing noun
things

A **thing** is something that is not a plant, an animal, or a human being.
জিনিস
What's that **thing** lying in the road?

think verb
thinks, thinking, thought

1 If you **think** something, you believe that it is true.
ভাবা
I **think** it's a great idea.

2 When you **think**, you use your mind.
চিন্তা করা
I tried to **think** what to do.

thirsty adjective
thirstier, thirstiest

If you are **thirsty**, you want to drink something.
তৃষ্ণার্ত

thought
⇨ Look at **think**.
I **thought** they were here.

thread noun
threads

Thread is a long, thin piece of cotton or wool that you use to sew cloth.
সুতো

three noun

Three is the number 3.
তিন

threw
⇨ Look at **throw**.
She **threw** her coat on to a chair.

throat noun
throats

1 Your **throat** is the back part of your mouth that you use to swallow and to breathe.
গলা

2 Your **throat** is also the front part of your neck.
টুঁটি

through

Through means going all the way from one side of something to the other side.
মধ্যে
We walked **through** the forest.

throw verb
throws, throwing, threw, thrown

When you **throw** something you are holding, you move your hand quickly and let the thing go, so that it moves through the air.
ছোঁড়া
Throw the ball to me.

thumb noun
thumbs

Your **thumb** is the short, thick finger on the side of your hand.
বুড়ো আঙুল
The baby sucked its **thumb**.

thunder noun

Thunder is the loud noise that you sometimes hear from the sky when there is a storm.
বজ্র

Thursday noun
Thursdays

Thursday is the day after Wednesday and before Friday.
বৃহস্পতিবার
I saw her on **Thursday**.

tidy - together

tidy *adjective*
tidier, tidiest

Something that is **tidy** is neat, with everything in its proper place.
পরিষ্কার পরিচ্ছন্ন

tie *verb*
ties, tying, tied

If you **tie** something, you fasten it with string or a rope.
বাঁধা

He **tied** the dog to the fence.

tie *noun*
ties

A **tie** is a long, narrow piece of cloth that you tie a knot in and wear around your neck with a shirt.
টাই

tiger *noun*
tigers

A **tiger** is a large wild cat that has orange fur with black stripes.
বাঘ

tight *adjective*
tighter, tightest

1. If clothes are **tight**, they are so small that they fit very close to your body.
আঁটসাঁট

   His trousers were very **tight**.

2. Something that is **tight** is fastened so that it is not easy to move it.
বাঁধা

   The string was tied in a **tight** knot.

time *noun*

1. **Time** is how long something takes to happen. We measure **time** in minutes, hours, days, weeks, months, and years.
সময়

   I've known him for a long **time**.

2. The **time** is a moment in the day that you describe in hours and minutes.
সময়

   "What **time** is it?"—"Ten past five."

tin *noun*
tins

1. **Tin** is a kind of soft, pale grey metal.
টিন

2. A **tin** is a metal container for food.
ধাতুর কৌটো

   She opened a **tin** of beans.

tiny *adjective*
tinier, tiniest

If something is **tiny**, it is very small.
ক্ষুদ্র

Our new kitten is **tiny**.

tired *adjective*

If you are **tired**, you need to rest or get some sleep.
ক্লান্ত

toad *noun*
toads

A **toad** is a small animal that looks like a frog. **Toads** have rough, dry skin and live on land.
ব্যাঙের মত একটি জন্তু

today

Today means the day that is happening now.
আজ

I feel much better **today**.

toe *noun*
toes

Your **toes** are the five parts at the end of each foot.
পায়ের আঙুল

I'm sorry I stood on your **toes**.

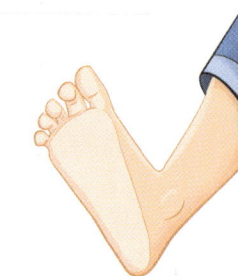

together

If people do something **together**, they do it with each other.
একসাথে

We played football **together**.

140

told
⇨ Look at **tell**.
We **told** them the answer.

tomato noun
tomatoes

A **tomato** is a soft red fruit with a lot of juice.
টমেটো

tomorrow
Tomorrow is the day after today.
আগামী কাল
I'll see you **tomorrow**.

tongue noun
tongues

Your **tongue** is the soft part inside your mouth that moves when you eat or talk.
জিভ

tonight
Tonight is the evening or night that will come at the end of today.
আজ রাত
We're going out **tonight**.

too
1 **Too** means also.
আরও
Can I come **too**?
2 You also use **too** to mean more than you want or need.
খুব বেশি
The TV is **too** loud.

took
⇨ Look at **take**.
It **took** me hours.

tool noun
tools

A **tool** is something that you hold in your hands and use to do a job.
যন্ত্র পাতি

tooth noun
teeth

1 Your **teeth** are the hard, white things in your mouth that you use to bite and chew food.
দাঁত
I clean my **teeth** twice a day.
2 The **teeth** of a comb, a saw, or a zip are the parts that are in a row along its edge.
ধারাল দাঁত

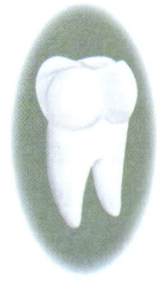

top noun
tops

1 The **top** of something is the highest part of it.
উঁচু অংশ
We climbed to the **top** of the hill.
2 The **top** of something is also the part that fits over the end of it.
ওপরের অংশ
He took the **top** off the jar.

tore
⇨ Look at **tear**.
She **tore** her dress on a nail.

torn
⇨ Look at **tear**.
He has **torn** the cover of the book.

tortoise noun
tortoises

A **tortoise** is an animal with a hard shell on its back. It can pull its head and legs inside the shell. **Tortoises** move very slowly.
কচ্ছপ

touch verb
touches, touching, touched

1 If you **touch** something, you put your fingers or your hand on it.
স্পর্শ করা
The baby **touched** my face.
2 If one thing **touches** another, they are so close that there is no space between them.
ছোঁয়া
Her feet **touched** the floor.

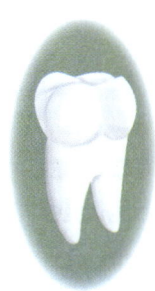

141

towards

Towards means in the direction of something.
অভিমুখে
He moved **towards** the door.

towel noun
towels

A **towel** is a piece of thick, soft cloth that you use to get yourself dry.
তোয়ালে

town noun
towns

A **town** is a place with a lot of streets, buildings, and shops, where people live and work.
শহর

toy noun
toys

A **toy** is something that you play with.
খেলনা

tractor noun
tractors

A **tractor** is a vehicle with big wheels at the back. **Tractors** are used on a farm to pull machines and other heavy things.
ট্র্যাক্টর

traffic noun

Traffic is all the vehicles that are on a road at the same time.
যানবাহন
There is a lot of **traffic** in the town today.

train noun
trains

A **train** is a long vehicle that is pulled by an engine along a railway line.
ট্রেন

travel verb
travels, travelling, travelled

When you **travel**, you go from one place to another.
ভ্রমণ করা
He **travelled** to many different countries.

tree noun
trees

A **tree** is a very tall plant with branches, leaves, and a hard main part that is called a trunk.
গাছ

triangle noun
triangles

1. A **triangle** is a shape with three straight sides.
   ত্রিভুজ
2. A **triangle** is also an instrument made of metal in the shape of a **triangle** that you hit with a stick to make music.
   ধাতুর বাদ্যযন্ত্র

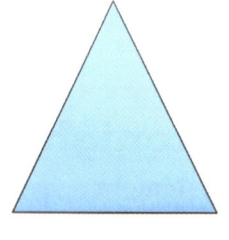

trick verb
tricks, tricking, tricked

If someone **tricks** you, they make you believe something that is not true so that you will do what they want.
চালাকি করা
They **tricked** her into giving them money.

tried

⇨ Look at **try**.
They **tried** their best.

tries

⇨ Look at **try**.
She **tries** to help.

trip - tunnel

trip noun
trips

When you go on a **trip**, you travel to a place and then come back.
ভ্রমণ
*We went on a **trip** to the park.*

trousers noun

Trousers are things that you can wear. They cover the part of your body below the waist, and each leg.
পাতলুন
*He was wearing brown **trousers**.*

truck noun
trucks

A **truck** is a large vehicle that is used to carry things.
ট্রাক

true adjective

1 If a story is **true**, it really happened.
সত্য
*Everything she said was **true**.*

2 If something is **true**, it is right or correct.
সঠিক
*Is it **true** that you have six cats?*

trunk noun
trunks

1 A **trunk** is the thick stem of a tree. The branches and roots grow from the **trunk**.
গাছের গুঁড়ি

2 An elephant's **trunk** is its long nose. Elephants use their **trunks** to suck up water and to lift things.
শুঁড়

3 A **trunk** is also a large, strong box that you use to keep things in.
টিনের বাক্স

try verb
tries, trying, tried

1 If you **try** to do something, you do it as well as you can.
চেষ্টা করা
*I will **try** to come tomorrow.*

2 If you **try** something, you test it to see what it is like or how it works.
পরীক্ষা করা
*Would you like to **try** my new bike?*

tube noun
tubes

1 A **tube** is a long, round, hollow piece of metal, rubber, or plastic.
নল
*The liquid goes through the **tube** into the bottle.*

2 A **tube** is also a soft metal or plastic container that you press to make what is in it come out.
টিউব
*He bought a **tube** of glue.*

Tuesday noun
Tuesdays

Tuesday is the day after Monday and before Wednesday.
মঙ্গলবার
*He came home on **Tuesday**.*

tune noun
tunes

A **tune** is a piece of music that is nice to listen to.
সুর
*She played a **tune** on the piano.*

tunnel noun
tunnels

A **tunnel** is a long hole that goes below the ground or through a hill.
সুড়ঙ্গ

143

turn - tyre

turn verb
turns, turning, turned

1. When you **turn**, you move in a different direction.
   ঘোরা
   He **turned** and walked away.
2. When something **turns**, it moves around in a circle.
   ঘুরে যাওয়া
   The wheels **turned** slowly.
3. If one thing **turns** into another thing, it becomes that thing.
   পরিণত হওয়া
   The tadpole **turned** into a frog.
4. When you **turn** a machine on, you make it start working. When you **turn** it off, you make it stop working.
   চালু করা/বন্ধ করা
   I **turned** off the television.

tusk noun
tusks

An elephant's **tusks** are the two very long, curved teeth that it has beside its trunk.
হাতির দাঁত

TV noun
TVs

TV is short for **television**.
টিভি
What's on **TV**?

twelve noun
Twelve is the number 12.
বারো

twice
If something happens **twice**, it happens two times.
দুবার
I've met him **twice**.

twig noun
twigs

A **twig** is a very small, thin branch that grows on a tree or a bush.
গাছের শাখা

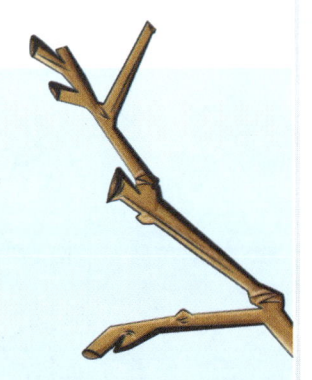

twin noun
twins

If two people are **twins**, they have the same parents and they were born on the same day. **Twins** often look alike.
যমজ

twist verb
twists, twisting, twisted

If you **twist** something, you turn one end of it in one direction while you hold the other end or turn it in the opposite direction.
পাক দেওয়া
She **twisted** the towel in her hands.

two noun
Two is the number 2.
দুই

tying
➡ Look at **tie**.
He was **tying** the two pieces of rope together.

type noun
types

A **type** of something is the kind of thing that it is.
প্রকার
Owls are a **type** of bird.

type verb
types, typing, typed

If you **type** something, you write it with a machine, for example a computer.
টাইপ করা
She **typed** a letter.

tyre noun
tyres

A **tyre** is a thick circle made of strong rubber that goes round a wheel. **Tyres** usually have air inside them.
টায়ার

Uu

ugly adjective
uglier, ugliest
If something is **ugly**, it is not nice to look at.
কুৎসিত
The monster had an **ugly** face.

umbrella noun
umbrellas
An **umbrella** is a long stick that is joined to a cover made of cloth or plastic. You hold an **umbrella** over your head so that you will not get wet in the rain.
ছাতা

uncle noun
uncles
Your **uncle** is the brother of your mother or father, or the husband of your aunt.
জ্যাঠা/খুড়া/মাতুল/পিসে/মেসো

understand verb
understands, understanding, understood
If you **understand** something, you know what it means or why or how it happens.
বুঝতে পারা
I didn't **understand** what he said.

underwear noun
Your **underwear** is the name for the clothes that you wear next to your skin, under all your other clothes.
অন্তর্বাস

undress verb
undresses, undressing, undressed
When you **undress**, you take off your clothes.
পোষাক খোলা

uniform noun
uniforms
A **uniform** is a special set of clothes that some people wear to show what job they do, or some children wear to show what school they go to.
ইউনিফর্ম
I put on my school **uniform**.

until
If something happens **until** a time, it happens before that time and then stops at that time.
যদবধি/না পর্যন্ত
Wait here **until** I come back.

unusual adjective
If something is **unusual**, it does not happen very often.
অস্বাভাবিক
It is **unusual** for him to be late.

up
When something moves **up**, it moves from a lower place to a higher place.
ওপরে
She ran **up** the stairs.

upon
Upon means the same as **on**.
ওপরে
He stood **upon** the bridge.

upset adjective
If you are **upset**, you are sad because something bad has happened.
বিচলিত
I was **upset** when my brother broke my doll.

upside down
1 If something is **upside down**, the part that is usually at the bottom is at the top.
নিচের অংশ ওপরের দিকে করা
The picture was **upside down**.
2 If you hang **upside down**, your head is below your feet.
ওপরের অংশ নিচের দিকে করা

urgent adjective
If something is **urgent**, it is very important and you need to do something about it quickly.
জরুরী
This problem is **urgent**.

use verb
uses, using, used
If you **use** something, you do something with it.
ব্যবহার করা
Use a cloth to clean the table.

useful adjective
If something is **useful**, you can use it to do something or to help you in some way.
দরকারী

usual adjective
Something that is **usual** is what happens most often.
সাধারণ
He arrived at his **usual** time.

usually
If something **usually** happens, it is the thing that happens most often.
সাধারণতঃ
I **usually** take the bus to school.

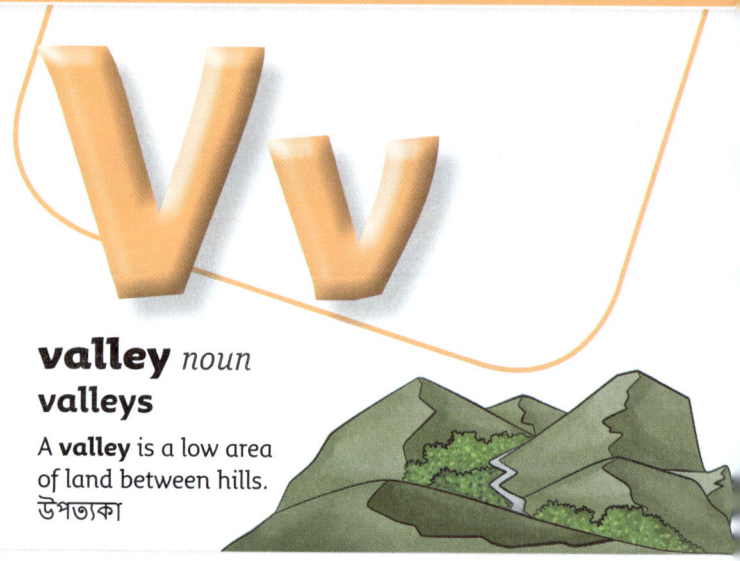

valley noun
valleys
A **valley** is a low area of land between hills.
উপত্যকা

valuable adjective
If something is **valuable**, it is worth a lot of money.
মূল্যবান

van noun
vans
A **van** is a covered vehicle larger than a car but smaller than a lorry. People use **vans** for carrying things.
ভ্যান গাড়ি

vase noun
vases
A **vase** is a jar for flowers.
ফুলদানি

vegetable noun
vegetables
Vegetables are plants that you can cook and eat.
সবজি

vehicle noun
vehicles
A **vehicle** is a machine that carries people or things from one place to another.
বাহন

verb noun
verbs
A **verb** is a word like 'sing,' 'feel,' or 'eat' that you use for saying what someone or something does.
ক্রিয়া

very - want

very

Very is used before a word to make it stronger.
খুব
*She had a **very** bad dream.*

vet noun
vets

A **vet** is a doctor for animals.
পশু-চিকিৎসক

video noun
videos

A **video** is a copy of a film or television programme.
ভিডিও

village noun
villages

A **village** is a small town.
গ্রাম

voice noun
voices

Your **voice** is the sound that comes from your mouth when you talk or sing.
কণ্ঠস্বর

volcano noun
volcanoes

A **volcano** is a mountain that throws out hot, liquid rock and fire.
আগ্নেয়গিরি

vote verb
votes, voting, voted

When a group of people **vote**, everybody shows what they want to do, usually by writing on a piece of paper or by putting their hands up.
ভোট দেওয়া

*We **voted** to send money to people who were in the earthquake.*

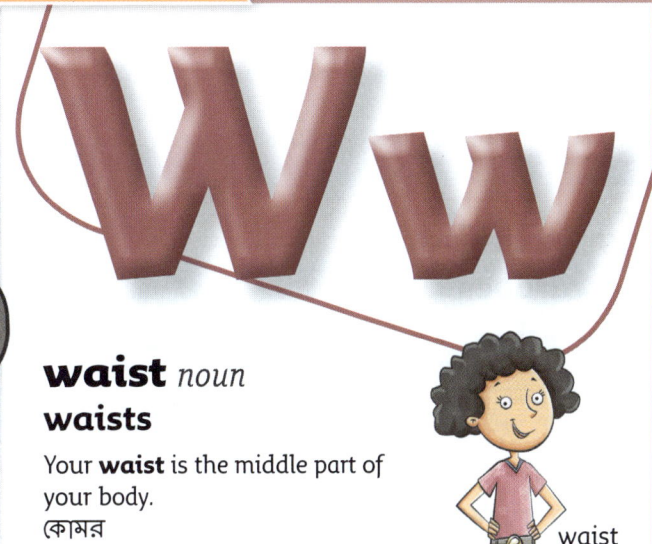

Ww

waist noun
waists

Your **waist** is the middle part of your body.
কোমর

waist

wait verb
waits, waiting, waited

When you **wait** for something or someone, you spend time doing very little, before something happens.
অপেক্ষা করা

wake verb
wakes, waking, woke, woken

When you **wake** up, you stop sleeping.
জেগে ওঠা

walk verb
walks, walking, walked

When you **walk**, you move along by putting one foot in front of the other.
হাঁটা

wall noun
walls

A **wall** is one of the sides of a building or a room.
দেওয়াল

want verb
wants, wanting, wanted

If you **want** something, you would like to have it.
চাওয়া

147

war - wave

war noun
wars

A **war** is when countries or groups fight each other.
যুদ্ধ

wardrobe noun
wardrobes

A **wardrobe** is a tall cupboard that you can hang your clothes in.
পোশাকের আলমারি

warm adjective
warmer, warmest

Something that is **warm** is not cold, but not hot.
উষ্ণ

The bread is still **warm** from the oven.

warn verb
warns, warning, warned

If you **warn** someone about a possible problem or danger, you tell them about it.
সতর্ক করা

I **warned** them not to go.

was
➡ Look at **be**.
It **was** my birthday yesterday.

wash verb
washes, washing, washed

If you **wash** something, you clean it using soap and water.
ধোওয়া

wasn't
Wasn't is short for **was not**.
ছিল না

She **wasn't** happy.

wasp noun
wasps

A **wasp** is an insect with wings and yellow and black stripes across its body. **Wasps** can sting people.
বোলতা

waste verb
wastes, wasting, wasted

If you **waste** time, money, or energy, you use too much of it on something that is not important.
অপচয় করা

It's important not to **waste** water.

watch verb
watches, watching, watched

If you **watch** something, you look at it for a period of time.
লক্ষ্য করা

watch noun
watches

A **watch** is a small clock that you wear on your wrist.
হাতঘড়ি

water noun

Water is a clear liquid that has no colour, taste or smell. It falls from clouds as rain.
জল

wave noun
waves

Waves on the surface of the sea are the parts that move up and down.
ঢেউ

The **waves** broke over the rocks.

wave verb
waves, waving, waved

If you **wave** your hand, you move it from side to side, usually to say hello or goodbye.
হাত নাড়ানো

148

wax noun
Wax is a soft material that melts when you make it hot. It is used to make crayons and candles.
মোম

way noun
ways
1 A **way** of doing something is how you do it.
উপায়
*This is the **way** to throw the ball.*
2 The **way** to a place is how you get there.
রাস্তা
*We're going the wrong **way**!*

weak adjective
weaker, weakest
If someone or something is **weak**, they are not strong.
দুর্বল
*When she spoke, her voice was **weak**.*

wear verb
wears, wearing, wore, worn
When you **wear** clothes, shoes or glasses, you have them on your body.
পরা
*What are you going to **wear** today?*

weather noun
The **weather** is what it is like outside, for example if it is raining or sunny.
আবহাওয়া
*What will the **weather** be like tomorrow?*

web noun
webs
1 The **Web** is made up of a very large number of websites all joined together. You can use it anywhere in the world to search for information.
ওয়েব
2 A **web** is the thin net made by a spider from a string that comes out of its body.
মাকড়সার জাল

website noun
websites
A **website** is a place on the Internet that gives you information.
ওয়েবসাইট
*Our school has a **website**.*

we'd
1 **We'd** is short for **we had**.
আমাদের ছিল
***We'd** left early in the morning.*
2 **We'd** is also short for **we would**.
আমাদের হবে
***We'd** like you to come with us.*

wedding noun
weddings
A **wedding** is when two people get married.
বিবাহ

Wednesday noun
Wednesdays
Wednesday is the day after Tuesday and before Thursday.
বুধবার

week noun
weeks
A **week** is a period of seven days.
সপ্তাহ
*This is the last **week** of the holidays.*

weekend noun
weekends
The **weekend** is the days at the end of the week, when you do not go to school or work.
সপ্তাহান্ত

weigh verb
weighs, weighing, weighed
If you **weigh** something or someone, you measure how heavy they are.
ওজন করা
*I **weigh** more than my brother.*

weight noun
The **weight** of a person or thing is how heavy they are.
ওজন
*What is your **weight** and height?*

well
better, best
If you do something **well**, you do it in a good way.
ভাল
*He draws **well**.*

well noun
A **well** is a deep hole in the ground from which people take water, oil or gas.
কুয়ো

we'll
We'll is short for **we will**.
আমরা করব
We'll come along later.

went
⇨ Look at **go**.
*They **went** to school.*

were
⇨ Look at **be**.
*They **were** at home yesterday.*

we're
We're is short for **we are**.
আমরা হই
We're late!

weren't
Weren't is short for **were not**.
ছিল না
*They **weren't** at school yesterday.*

west noun
The **west** is the direction ahead of you when you are looking towards the place where the sun goes down.
পশ্চিম দিক

wet adjective
wetter, wettest
If something is **wet**, it is covered in water.
ভিজে

we've
We've is short for **we have**.
আমাদের আছে
We've got lots of books.

whale noun
whales
Whales are very large sea mammals.
তিমি
Whales breathe through a hole on the top of their heads.

what
You use **what** in questions when you ask for information.
কি?
What time is it?

wheat noun
Wheat is a crop. People make flour and bread from **wheat**.
গম

wheel noun
wheels
Wheels are round and they turn. Bikes and cars move along on **wheels**.
চাকা

wheelchair noun
wheelchairs
A **wheelchair** is a chair with wheels that you use if you cannot walk.
হুইলচেয়ার

when
You use **when** to ask what time something happened or will happen.
কখন?
When are you leaving?

where - wife

where

You use **where** to ask questions about the place something is in.
কোথায়?
***Where's** your house?*

which

You use **which** when you want help to choose between things.
কোন?
***Which** shoes should I put on?*

while

If one thing happens **while** another thing is happening, the two things are happening at the same time.
যখন
*She goes to work **while** her children are at school.*

whisper *verb*
whispers, whispering, whispered

When you **whisper**, you speak in a very quiet voice.
ফিসফিস করা
*Don't you know it's rude to **whisper**?*

whistle *verb*
whistles, whistling, whistled

When you **whistle**, you make sounds like music by blowing hard.
শিস্ দেওয়া

white *noun*

White is the colour of snow or milk.
সাদা
*His shirt is **white**.*

who

You use **who** in questions when you ask about someone's name.
কে
***Who** won the quiz?*

who'd

Who'd is short for **who would**.
কে করবে?
***Who'd** like to come with me?*

whole *adjective*

The **whole** of something is all of it.
গোটা
*Have the **whole** cake.*

who'll

Who'll is short for **who will**.
কে করবে?
***Who'll** go and find her?*

whose

You use **whose** to ask who something belongs to.
কার
***Whose** bag is this?*

why

You use **why** when you are asking about the reason for something.
কেন
***Why** did you do it?*

wide *adjective*
wider, widest

Something that is **wide** is a large distance from one side to the other.
চওড়া
*The bed is too **wide** for this room.*

width *noun*

The **width** of something is the distance from one side to another.
প্রস্থ
*Measure the full **width** of the table.*

wife *noun*
wives

A man's **wife** is the woman he is married to.
স্ত্রী

151

wild *adjective*
wilder, wildest

Wild animals or plants live or grow in nature, and people do not take care of them.
বন্য

will *verb*

You use **will** to talk about things that are going to happen in the future.
হবে
Mum will be angry.

win *verb*
wins, winning, won

If you **win**, you do better than everyone.
জেতা
You've won first prize!

wind *noun*

Wind is air that moves.
বাতাস

wind *verb*
winds, winding, wound

1. If a road or river **winds**, it twists and turns.
ঘুরে যাওয়া
2. When you **wind** something long around something, you wrap it around several times.
ঘুরিয়ে বাঁধা
She wound the rope around her waist.

window *noun*
windows

A **window** is a space in the wall of a building or in the side of a vehicle that has glass in it.
জানালা

wing *noun*
wings

The **wings** of birds, insects or aeroplanes are the parts that keep them in the air.
ডানা

winner *noun*
winners

The **winner** of a race or competition is the person who wins it.
বিজয়ী
Our teacher will give the prizes to the winners.

winter *noun*
winters

Winter is the season after autumn and before spring. In the **winter** the weather is usually cold.
শীতকাল

wipe *verb*
wipes, wiping, wiped

If you **wipe** dirt or liquid from something, you remove it using a cloth or your hands.
মোছা
She wiped the tears from her eyes.

wire *noun*
wires

A **wire** is a long thin piece of metal.
তার
The birds were sitting on a telephone wire.

wise *adjective*
wiser, wisest

A **wise** person can decide on the right thing to do.
জ্ঞানী

wish *verb*
wishes, wishing, wished

If you **wish** something, you would like it to be true.
মনোবাসনা
I wish I had a pet.

witch *noun*
witches

In children's stories, a **witch** is a woman who has magic powers that she uses to do bad things.
ডাইনি

152

with

1 If one person is **with** another, they are together in one place.
সঙ্গে
He's watching a film **with** his friends.

2 You use **with** to say that someone has something.
সহ
My daughter is the girl **with** brown hair.

without

If you do something **without** someone, they are not in the same place as you are, or they are not doing the same thing as you.
ছাড়া
He went **without** me.

wives

⇨ Look at **wife**.
The men bought flowers for their **wives**.

wizard noun
wizards

In children's stories, a **wizard** is a man who has magic powers.
যাদুকর

woke

⇨ Look at **wake**.
They **woke** early.

woken

⇨ Look at **wake**.
We were **woken** by a loud noise.

wolf noun
wolves

A **wolf** is a wild animal that looks like a large dog.
নেকড়ে

woman noun
women

A **woman** is an adult female person.
মহিলা

won

⇨ Look at **win**.
She **won** first prize.

won't

Won't is short for **will not**.
হবে না
I **won't** be late.

wood noun
woods

1 **Wood** is the hard material that trees are made of.
কাঠ

2 A **wood** is a large area of trees growing near each other.
জঙ্গল

wool noun

Wool is a material made from the fur of sheep. It is used for making things such as clothes.
পশম

word noun
words

Words are things that you say or write.
শব্দ
Some **words** are short and some are long.

wore

⇨ Look at **wear**.
She **wore** a red dress.

work verb
works, working, worked

1 When you **work**, you do something that uses a lot of your time or effort.
কাজ করা
We **work** hard all day.

2 If a machine **works**, it does its job.
ঠিকঠাক চলা
The TV isn't **working**.

world - wrong

world noun
worlds

The **world** is the earth, the planet we live on.
পৃথিবী

worm noun
worms

A **worm** is a small animal with a long thin body, no bones, and no legs.
কেঁচো

worn
➡ Look at **wear**.
Have you **worn** this?

worry verb
worries, worrying, worried

If you **worry**, you keep thinking about problems that you have or about nasty things that might happen.
চিন্তা করা

worse
If something is **worse** than another thing, it is not as good.
খারাপ
My spelling is **worse** than yours.

worst
If something is the **worst**, all other things are better.
সবথেকে খারাপ
That was the **worst** day in my life.

worth
If something is **worth** a sum of money, that's how much you could sell it for.
মূল্য
This gold ring is **worth** a lot of money.

would verb
You use **would** to say that someone agreed to do something. You use **would not** to say that they refused to do something.
হবে
They said they **would** come to my party.

wound
➡ Look at **wind**.
She **wound** the rope around her wrist.

wrap verb
wraps, wrapping, wrapped

When you **wrap** something, you fold paper or cloth around it to cover it.
মোড়া
I didn't have enough paper to **wrap** the present.

wrist noun
wrists

Your **wrist** is the part of your body between your arm and your hand. Your **wrists** bend when you move your hands.
কবজি

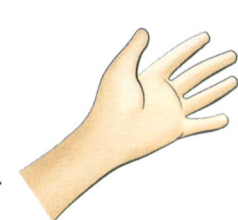

write verb
writes, writing, wrote, written

When you **write** something, you use a pen or pencil to make letters, words, or numbers.
লেখা
He **wrote** his name in the book.

writing noun
Writing is words that have been written or printed.
লেখা
Can you read my **writing**?

written
➡ Look at **write**.
My uncle has **written** a song.

wrong adjective
1 If you say that an answer is **wrong**, you mean that it is not right.
ভুল
No, you've got that **wrong**!

2 If you say that something someone does is **wrong**, you mean that it is bad.
অন্যায়
It is **wrong** to hurt animals.

Xx

X-ray noun
X-rays

An **X-ray** is a picture of the inside of someone's body.
এক্স-রে
The **X-ray** showed that my arm was broken.

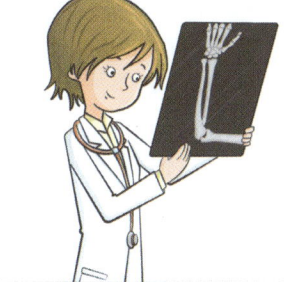

xylophone noun
xylophones

A **xylophone** is an instrument made of flat pieces of wood or metal in a row. You hit the pieces with a stick to make different sounds.
জাইলোফোন

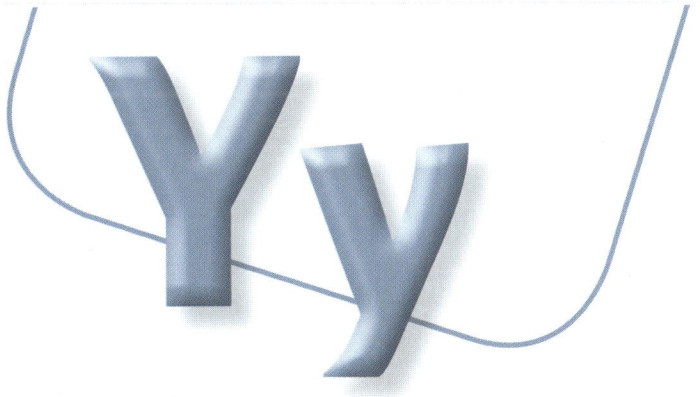

Yy

yacht noun
yachts

A **yacht** is a large boat with sails or an engine, used for races or for making trips.
প্রমোদতরণী

yawn verb
yawns, yawning, yawned

If you **yawn**, you open your mouth very wide and breathe in more air than usual because you are tired or bored.
হাই তোলা

year noun
years

A **year** is a period of twelve months, beginning on January 1 and finishing on December 31.
বৎসর

yell verb
yells, yelling, yelled

If you **yell**, you shout something, often because you are angry.
রেগে চিৎকার করা
She **yelled** at him to stop.

yellow noun

Yellow is the colour of lemons or butter.
হলুদ
Her favourite colour is **yellow**.

yes

You say **yes** to agree with someone or to say that something is true, or if you want something.
হ্যাঁ!

yesterday

Yesterday is the day before today.
গতকাল
There was no school **yesterday**.

yogurt or **yoghurt** noun
yogurts or yoghurts

Yogurt is a thick liquid food that is made from milk.
দই
I like strawberry **yogurt** more than peach **yogurt**.

yolk noun
yolks

The **yolk** of an egg is the yellow part.
ডিমের কুসুম

you

You means the person or people that someone is talking or writing to.
তুমি
Can I help **you**?

155

you'd

you'd

1 **You'd** is short for **you had**.
আপনার/তোমার ছিল
I thought **you'd** told him.

2 **You'd** is also short for **you would**.
আপনি/তুমি করবেন/করবে
You'd like it a lot.

you'll

You'll is short for **you will**.
আপনি/তুমি হবেন/হবে
You'll be late!

young *adjective*
younger, youngest

A **young** person, animal, or plant has not lived for very long.
অল্পবয়সী
A kitten is a **young** cat.

your

You use **your** to show that something belongs to the people that you are talking to.
আপনার/তোমার
I do like **your** name.

you're

You're is short for **you are**.
আপনি/তুমি হন/হও
You're very early!

yours

Yours refers to something belonging to the people that you are talking to.
আপনার
His hair is longer than **yours**.

yourself
yourselves

Yourself means you alone.
আপনি/তুমি নিজে
You'll hurt **yourself**.

you've

You've is short for **you have**.
You've got very long legs.

Zz

zebra *noun*
zebras

A **zebra** is a wild African animal like a horse with black and white stripes.
জেব্রা

zero
zeros or **zeroes**

Zero is the number 0.
শূন্য

zip *noun*
zips

A **zip** is two long rows of little teeth and a piece that slides along them. You pull this to open or close the **zip**.
জিপ

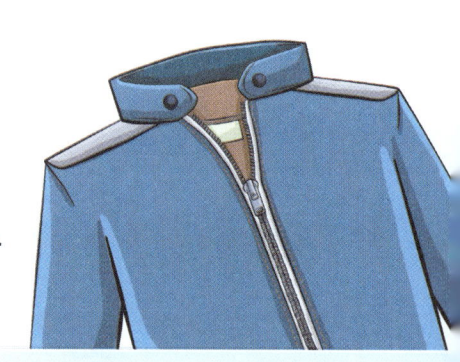

zoo *noun*
zoos

A **zoo** is a place where live animals are kept so that people can look at them.
চিড়িয়াখানা